The HIGH CALL *of* FOR GIVENESS
It's a Mandate

Leader Guide

Rosemarie Downer, Ph.D.

The High Call of Forgiveness
Leader Guide

by

Rosemarie Downer, Ph.D.

Copyright © 2021

ISBN: 9798544996170

Scripture quotations marked (KJV) are taken from the Holy Bible, King James Version, Cambridge, 1769. Used by permission. All rights reserved.

Scripture quotations marked (MSG) are taken from The Message. Copyright © 1993, 1994, 1995, 1996, 2000, 2001, 2002. Used by permission of NavPress Publishing Group.

Scripture quotations marked (NIV) are taken from the Holy Bible, New International Version®, NIV®. Copyright © 1973, 1978, 1984 by Biblica, Inc.™ Used by permission of Zondervan. All rights reserved worldwide. www.zondervan.com.

Scripture quotations marked (NKJV) are taken from the New King James Version. Copyright © 1982 by Thomas Nelson, Inc. Used by permission. All rights reserved.

This book is designed to provide accurate and authoritative information regarding the subject matter covered. However, this information is given with the understanding that the author is engaged in rendering legal or professional advice.

About the Author

Dr. Rosemarie Downer is a dedicated follower of Christ who aspires to having the closest relationship with Christ possible. Her service in the body of Christ primarily involves teaching and preaching. She also spent well over 30 years serving in youth ministries. Other focus areas in her ministry include women and single adults. As well, she often ministers on issues that address emotional healing and well-being. She counts every opportunity to minister an ultimate privilege from God the Father and does not take it lightly.

She is the founder and former President of BRYDGES (Building Responsible Youth by Delivering Genuine Enrichment Services), over which she functioned as the President for 15 years – 2001 through 2016. She is a published author of The Self-Scarred Church and several parenting handbooks. Additionally, she is the author of a comprehensive ministry development course – Find and Occupy Your Place and the Continuum of Care Youth Ministry Development Handbook.

Dr. Downer served at The U.S. Department of Agriculture as a social science researcher for 20 years and as an adjunct professor at Bowie State University for 24 years. She is now retired from both positions and is currently a private consultant doing research and evaluation and doing what she dreamed of doing for years, and that is to write books to edify the body of Christ.

The pivotal scripture verse for her ministry is 3John 2 – "*Beloved, I wish above all things that thou mayest prosper and be in health, even as thy soul prospereth.*" Her most favorite Bible verse is Philippians 1:6: "*Being confident of this very thing, that he which hath begun a good work in you will perform it until the day of Jesus Christ.*" Her favorite Bible character is Moses because he had the relationship with Abba Father that she so very deeply desires. Moses was able to talk to God the Father face-to-face and without riddle because of the close relationship he had with Him. That is her desire!

Contents

Overview of Lesson Series

The order in which the lessons are presented lines up directly with the chapters in *The High Call of Forgiveness*. The leader guide contains answers to the questions in the lessons, and the student workbook contains space for the students to write their answers.

The lessons are designed to encourage discussions, close examination of scripture, and the application of the Word. The lessons also encourage further study of the Word beyond what is presented in the book. Each session ends with suggested prayer targets and a reflection and personal application exercise.

Who Will Benefit from *The High Call of Forgiveness* Lessons?

This lesson series will benefit both the facilitator and the students. It will benefit anyone who has a desire to please the Lord. It will particularly help anyone who is offended and is struggling with unforgiveness. People could also benefit vicariously from the lessons. As students learn from the lesson series, they could inspire others who are offended but are finding it difficult to forgive. In addition, counselors and therapists, as well as pastors and ministerial staff persons can use the High Call of Forgiveness lesson series when counseling anyone who is challenged by unforgiveness or is hurting due to an infraction against them.

Tips for the Leader

Lesson facilitators are encouraged to do the following:

1. Pray before each session and remain prayerful about the participants throughout the series.

2. Read the book *The High Call of Forgiveness* before starting the sessions. As the facilitator, you may read the entire book before starting the sessions or read the chapter that aligns with each lesson before facilitating each session.

3. Think through the discussion questions ahead of time. Have some scenarios and probing questions prepared.

4. Ensure that you have resolved all personal issues of offense. You want to make sure you are teaching from your spirit and not your intellect. If you are clear of offense, your

teaching will be much more effective than if you are teaching one thing but living the opposite.

5. Read each lesson before attempting to teach it. Read the answer to each question and determine if you have anything to add.

6. Be prepared for questions from the participants. They will ask questions at times about specific situations. Be careful not to give a generic response to specific situations for which you do not have full details. You do not want the participants to take an answer to a specific situation and apply it to general circumstances.

7. Be sure to have additional answers of your own in places where additional responses are solicited. You want to be prepared, just in case the participants do not have anything to add.

8. Be prepared to pray with and counsel the participants outside of the teaching sessions.

Tips for the Students

1. Read the book *The High Call of Forgiveness* before starting the sessions. You may read the entire book before starting the sessions or read the chapter that aligns with each lesson before each respective session.

2. To get the fullest benefit of the lessons, be prayerful as you go through the series, and be honest with yourself. God already knows your heart, but He wants you to be honest with Him about where you are.

3. Pray the suggested prayer points provided at the end of each lesson.

4. Complete all reflection and personal application exercises.

Book Chapters and Workbook Sessions Alignment

Workbook Sessions	Book Chapters
Unit 1: The Context of Offense	
1. The Strategy of the Enemy	1. It's A Strategy
2. Offense Is a Kingdom Matter	2. Offense Must Come
3. Offense Is Inevitable	2. Offense Must Come
4. Nothing Just Happens	3. But God Has a Plan
5. Permission to Hurt	4. Hurt Is Okay
Unit 2: The Snare of Unforgiveness	
6. Say Yes, Forgive	5. Forgiveness Is a Mandate
7. It's a Lie	6. Do Not Believe the Lies
8. The Ties That Bind to Unforgiveness	7. Self, The Tie That Binds to Unforgiveness
9. It's A Trap	8. The Costs of Unforgiveness
10. The Costs of Unforgiveness (Part 1)	8. The Costs of Unforgiveness
11. The Costs of Unforgiveness (Part 2)	8. The Costs of Unforgiveness
12. Beyond Unforgiveness	9. Is Anything Worse Than Unforgiveness?
Unit 3: The Liberty of Forgiveness	
13. Forgiveness God's Way (Part 1)	10. The Rewards of Forgiveness
14. Forgiveness God's Way (Part 2)	10. The Rewards of Forgiveness
Unit 4: The Rewards of Forgiveness	
15. It's Blessed to Forgive	10. The Rewards of Forgiveness
16. Beyond Forgiveness	11. Beyond Forgiveness: Reconciliation
Unit 5: His Grace Is Enough	
17. You Can Do It!	12. We Can If Christ Lives in Us
18. God Wants You Whole	13. Practical Steps to Healing

Figure 1

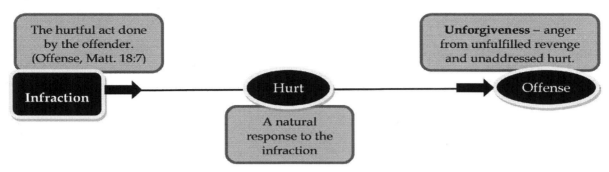

Figure 2

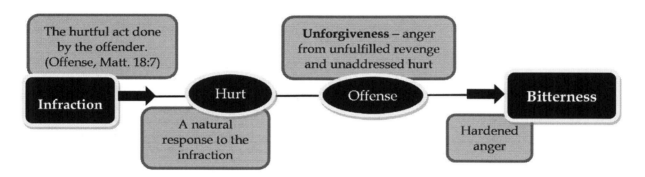

Figure 3

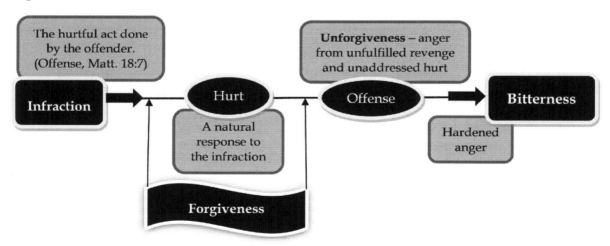

Unit 1: The Context of Offense

Session 1: The Strategy of the Enemy

One cannot randomly execute a device; it must be sensibly planned for it to be effective. So, the first thing we must note is that Satan plans carefully before he attacks.

Session Goals

By the end of this session, participants will

- identify the strategies we can use against the enemy,
- complete a review of the prayer Jesus prayed for us and how Satan sets out to block it, and
- have a better understanding of the capabilities of the enemy of our souls.

Know Your Enemy

Boxing is a sport that I personally think is barbaric, but there is much to be learned from it. I honestly do not see how a sport could be entertaining when the intent is to do as much damage as possible to your opponent. The objective of this sport is to hit your opponent hard enough and give him or her so hard a beating that he or she is then rendered unconscious. But none of this will happen — in fact, you will be the one beaten to unconsciousness — if you do not study your opponent.

1. Second Corinthians 2:11 tells us three things:
   a) **Know your enemy, Satan.**
   b) **Satan has devices.**
   c) **If we don't know the devices of our enemy, he will take advantage of us.**

Lest Satan should get an advantage of us: for we are not ignorant of his devices.
—2 Corinthians 2:11 KJV

2. Second Corinthians 2:11 says that Satan has devices. What is a device?
A scheme, a trick, or a ploy.

What Is a Scheme?

A scheme can be defined as a **systematic plan**. *Merriam-Webster's Dictionary* defines *scheme* as "a clever and often dishonest plan to do or get something."

> *The Scripture is clear that Satan is as an enemy of God and therefore, an enemy of God's people. Satan has many names, including, the Devil, the Dragon, the Serpent, Enemy, Tempter, Murderer, Father of Lies, Adversary, Accuser, Destroyer, and the Evil One.*

If the devil has devices, it means he is carefully planning against us. His attacks are not random. They are well thought out. If he is planning against us, we should be planning against him. To plan effectively against the devil, we must know how he operates. We cannot pretend he doesn't exist. We make a huge mistake when we underestimate his capabilities.

The truth is — Satan is far cleverer than most people imagine. He is very influential in the earth and has scored with even the most learned and intellectual people of this world — sometimes even the most spiritual people. To put the matter simply, Satan's most widely used strategy is to prompt us and everyone in the world to believe that he is not Satan. He wants us to believe that he means us well. This is a lie!

He manipulates us to accept this lie about him by subtly introducing his venomous ideologies to us. Many of us have subscribed to his ways and have come to believe something quite different from the truth about him. Satan wants us to believe that he is a righteous spirit being who means us well. He wants us to believe that we can succeed and be prosperous if we do things his way.

But remember, he is the father of lies. The truth is that Satan is here to kill our dreams and destinies. He has come to kill, steal, and destroy (John 10:10). Jesus, our Savior, accurately called Satan a murderer from the beginning (John 8:44). He goes about as a roaring lion, seeking to devour whomever he can (1 Peter 5:8) and he wants us to believe otherwise. Unfortunately, he has managed to pull off this great trick with many — the greatest trick ever conceived in the history of the world.

Satan does not want us to know the truth about him, but we must know how he operates. In knowing our enemy, we must take these steps:

3. Identify what he does well.
   a) 2 Corinthians 11:13–14; Revelation 12:9; 20:3; 1 Timothy 3:7; 2 Timothy 2:26—**Deceives.**
   b) 1 Peter 5:8—**Seeks to devour us. He is our adversary.**

c) Identify a few other things that Satan does well along with the Scripture references.

4. Know what strategies work against him. Discuss how each of these strategies defies Satan:

a) Ephesians 6:11— **Put on the whole armor of God**.

b) Ephesians 6:14— **Waist girded with truth, breastplate of righteousness.**

c) Ephesians 6:15— **Feet covered with the preparation of the gospel of peace.**

d) Ephesians 6:16— **Shield of faith.**

e) Ephesians 6:17— **Helmet of salvation and the sword of the Spirit.**

f) Ephesians 6:18— **Prayer.**

g) Ephesians 6:19— **Share the gospel of Jesus Christ.**

h) Revelation 19:10— **Testifying of Jesus.**

5. Determine how our strengths/weaknesses match up with the devil's.

a) 1 John 4:4— **Christ in us is greater than Satan**.

b) Romans 8:37— **We are more than conquerors**.

c) Philippians 4:13— **We can do all things through Christ**.

d) Isaiah 40:29— **God gives strength to the weak**.

> Ye are of God, little children, and have overcome them: because greater is he that is in you, than he that is in the world.
> —1John 4:4 (KJV)
>
> Nay, in all these things we are more than conquerors through him that loved us.
> Romans 8:37 (KJV)
>
> I can do all things through Christ which strengtheneth me.
> Philippians 4:13 (KJV)
>
> He gives strength to the weary and increases the power of the weak.
> Isaiah 40:29 (NIV)

Second Corinthians 2:11 also tells us not to be ignorant:

The devil can only know what we disclose or expose to him, and we do this primarily through the words we speak.

6. The Greek word for *ignorant* is *agnoeo*. The meaning of agnoeo is "**without knowledge or understanding of**."

7. The English word *agnostic* (unsure, uncertain, doubting) is derived from agnoeo. The word *ignore* also comes from agnoeo. Therefore, we are admonished in 2 Corinthians 2:11 not to **ignore** or not to lack understanding or wisdom of the strategies of Satan, because if we do, he is likely to get the better of us.

8. The Greek word for *device* is *noéma*, meaning **purpose** or **the intellect**. Satan's devices are purposeful; they are goal oriented, and he uses intelligence to design and execute them. His intelligence is what he learns about us. But the devil can only know what we disclose or expose to him, and we do this primarily through the words we speak.

9. What are some attributes of Satan?

a) John 8:44— **Liar. He is the father of lies**.
b) John 8:44— **Murderer. He was a murderer from the beginning**.
c) Matthew 4:3— **Tempter**.
d) Revelation 12:10— **Accuser**.
e) Matthew 13:19— **Thief**.
f) John 10:10— **Thief, murderer, destroyer.**
g) Identify a few more attributes of Satan along with the scripture references.

Think of a time when you experienced any of these attributes of Satan in your personal life.

➢ *Discuss how Satan lies to us, kills things in our lives, and tempts us. Encourage the participants to share the strategies they use to overcome the tactics of the enemy. Ask them...*
  • Has Satan lied to you?
  • Has he killed or tried to kill anything in your life?
  • Has he tempted you?
  • Has he ever accused you?
➢ *Now identify and discuss occasions when the Church (the people of God as a unit) experienced Satan as a liar, a murderer, a tempter, or an accuser.*

> The tempter came to him and said, "If you are the Son of God, tell these stones to become bread."
> —Matthew 4:3 (NIV)
>
> And I heard a loud voice saying in heaven, Now is come salvation, and strength, and the kingdom of our God, and the power of his Christ: for the accuser of our brethren is cast down, which accused them before our God day and night.
> —Revelation 12:10 (KJV)

Satan, our enemy, is deliberate about his attacks:
  • He plans carefully before making an attack.
  • He does nothing without a goal in mind.
  • He is not senseless.
  • He attacks with a target and with a fixed intent.
  • He takes time to study us before he moves in.
  • He is in no hurry to attack. After careful study, he is better informed about the vulnerable places in our lives, and then he attacks.

> *Satan waited forty long days to tempt Jesus. He is doing the same today. Our prayers, fasting, worship, and all our other religious activities do not deter him. He is patient. He can wait until we are done.*

Satan the Opportunist

Satan attacks in every area where he gets an opportunity. He will wreak havoc in every area of our lives that is not sealed off by the Holy Spirit. In this case, we are talking about offense. He will cause offense in any place we are not guarded.

Offense originates in hurt, which can only occur in the context of relationships or any level of interaction with other people. An inanimate object cannot hurt us; it requires people to cause hurt that could ultimately lead to offense. Therefore, any relationship with any level of fragility is an open invitation for offense to occur.

We should also note that Satan cannot attack unless we give him the opportunity. He will cause offense in any relationship in which we give him an opening. This could be with extended family, in parent-child relationships, at work, with spouses, or even in relationships with the members of the body of Christ: brothers, sisters, and leaders alike.

Satan Never Misses an Opportunity

> Above all else, guard your heart, for everything you do flows from it.
> —Proverbs 4:23 (NIV)
>
> 25 Wherefore putting away lying, speak every man truth with his neighbour: for we are members one of another. 26 Be ye angry, and sin not: let not the sun go down upon your wrath: 27 Neither give place to the devil.
> —Ephesians 4:25-27 (KJV)

10.   Satan will cause offense in any area of our lives that is not **sealed** off by the **Holy Spirit**.

11.   Proverbs 4:23— How can we seal off every opening in our lives? We must **guard** our heart with all **diligence**.

12. Satan will cause offense in any relationship in which we give him an **opening**.

13. Ephesians 4:25-27— **Lying and anger** can give Satan the opportunity to work against us.

14. Identify some other openings that can give Satan an opportunity to work against us.
    a) Genesis 3:6— **Disobedience, focus on self**
    b) 1 John 2:16— **Lust and pride**
    c) 2 Samuel 11:2-10— **Lack of self-control, negligence**

Jesus Prayed to Block the Opportunist

Jesus knew that Satan is an opportunist, and that is why He prayed as He did in John 17.

15. Jesus prayed a very intense prayer for His disciples and for **those who will believe in Him through the disciples' message** (John 17:20).

16. That includes all believers of Christ who would come after the **disciples**. That includes **us**. That includes **me**.

17. Jesus prayed that we would be one so that **the world may believe that God sent Him** (John 17: 23).

> *The presence of offense in the Body of Christ leaves us with only a form of godliness, but no power to make disciples.*

18. Jesus prayed that the world would know that His Father loves them the **same way His Father loves Him**.

19. Ultimately, when the church is not united, our capacity to make **disciples** is compromised.

➤ *Discuss how a divided church compromises our ability to effectively make disciples.*

Satan Is Aware of Jesus's Prayer

20. He knows that the **unity** of the church will tell the world that Christ died for them.

21. He knows that the unity of the church conveys the **love** of God to the world.

22. He causes **division** by way of **offense** to make the church ineffective in winning the lost to Christ.

> [20] My prayer is not for them alone. I pray also for those who will believe in me through their message [21] that all of them may be one, Father, just as you are in me and I am in you. May they also be in us so that the world may believe that you have sent me. [22] I have given them the glory that you gave me, that they may be one as we are one—[23] I in them and you in me—so that they may be brought to complete unity. Then the world will know that you sent me and have loved them even as you have loved me.
> —John 17:20-23 (NIV)

Satan's Impending Doom

The spirit being we know today as Satan was called Lucifer in heaven. The Bible tells us that he is a created being. He was a cherub, both beautiful and fearfully awesome (Ezekiel 1:7–24). God is sovereign over everything. He is the ultimate ruler, but He does not take away the will to choose from His creation. Hence, Lucifer had free will. God did not create Lucifer as evil but having free will, gave Lucifer the potential for sin. Free will reveals the character of a person. Our choices reflect the passion of our hearts, which in turn defines our true characters.

> *We can say that Satan's defeat has already transpired. The crucifixion and resurrection of Christ assured Satan's doom.*

God cannot sin, and it is His desire that none would sin (2 Peter 3:9), but He does not take the capacity to sin from His creation. Having free will, Lucifer chose to rebel. He was the first to ever sin, so he became the author of sin. This evil is the result of a free-will choice that was made by Lucifer. Pride and envy caused Lucifer to erupt major division in heaven, and God would not have it; so, the battle in the spiritual realm between Lucifer and God began.

Satan is the ultimate deceiver. He is most proficient at making rebellion look attractive. He is the genius of doubt and the originator of lying. He deceived Eve in the garden of Eden by imperceptibly challenging the Word of God, and he has been working diligently ever since to assault the minds and hearts of humanity.

This battle between God (His people) and Satan is still happening today. We are in a war. Second Corinthians 10:3b (KJV) tells us *"we do not war according to the flesh"* but are engaged in a spiritual battle. The one that is waging the war is none other than Satan himself.

But despite what Satan is doing today, his demise was predicted from the very beginning. In Genesis 3:15, God prophesied that the serpent (Satan) would bruise the heel of the Seed of the woman, but Jesus — the Seed of the woman — would crush the serpent's head. We can say that Satan's defeat has already transpired. The crucifixion and resurrection of Christ assured Satan's doom.

The inevitable awaits Satan and all the enemies of God. They will be thrown into the lake of fire for all eternity. They will be tormented day and night forever and ever (See Revelation 14:11 and 20:10).

The Bible is explicit. There will be no relief for Satan and the enemies of God. There is not even an end in sight for this eternal torment. This unending suffering is recompense for their sins against the one true and infinitely holy God.

Revelation 20:1-3, 10 gives an account of Satan's disposition.

23.   Satan will be bound and will be cast into a **bottomless** pit.

24.   He will be **shut up**, and his dominion on the earth will be **terminated** so that he can no longer deceive the nations.

25. His destination is the **lake** of **fire** and **brimstone**, where he will be tormented **day** and **night**, for ever and ever.

End the session with prayer. Suggested prayer points:

1. A keen awareness of the strategies and devices of Satan.

2. The faith and confidence to recognize, activate, and walk in the power that resides in you. If you are not a follower of Christ, ask Jesus to come into your heart. After accepting Him, He will live inside you. The promise that *"greater is he that is in you, than he that is in the world"* (1 John 4:4) will become your promise as well.

3. Wisdom to detect Satan's lies and deceptions and the power to resist his temptations.

4. Power to live a life that gives Satan no opportunity or opening to work against you. Pray against disobedience, pride, lying, anger, lust, and lack of self-control, and anything else that is against the nature of God that comes to your mind.

Reflection and Personal Application

Think about the area(s) of your life where you struggle most. It could be fear, doubt, anxiety, ungratefulness, low self-esteem, lack of temperance, uncontrolled anger, over-sensitivity — anything.

Ask God to show you the devices and strategies that Satan is using against you to make this a challenge for you. Likewise, ask God to show you the opening that has been created in your life to give Satan this advantage over you.

As God reveals these things to you, write them down, and make them the foci of your prayers until you get a breakthrough. Be diligent in prayer. Do not stop praying until you have overcome. If needed, consider talking to a brother or sister in Christ who is stronger than you in the area in which you are struggling.

> By way of offense, Satan's objective is to keep us churchy but powerless, making our message of no effect.

Session Goals

By the end of this session, participants will

- understand the larger plan behind offense,
- understand that offense in the church is not a personal matter but a kingdom matter, and
- understand that every member of the body of Christ is important to the functioning of the body.

It's Not about You

> *His objective is to keep us churchy but powerless, making our message of no effect.*

Offense is linked to hurt, pain, and broken relationships, which are manifested in disunity or lack of oneness. By causing offense in the Church, Satan can accomplish his goal of dividing us and hindering us from winning the lost to Christ. By winning the lost to Christ, we reduce the number of victimized souls Satan can take with him to his eternal fate, and that is the very opposite of what he wants. He knows that if he gets one member of the body, he can make progress toward accomplishing his larger agenda, which is to take as many as he can with him to his impending doom. His objective is to keep us churchy but powerless, making our message of no effect.

1. What is Satan's goal when he causes offense among brothers and sisters in Christ? <u>**Divide the church. Dissipate the love of Christ among us. Make our preaching of the gospel of no effect. Take our focus off kingdom matters.**</u>

 2. Why would a person who is hurt by a fellow believer think they were targeted by the brother or sister? **Because the person doesn't understand the strategies of the enemy. Because self is not crucified.**

> "The King will reply, 'Truly I tell you, whatever you did for one of the least of these brothers and sisters of mine, you did for me."
> —Matthew 25:40 (NIV)

3. What evidence is there that when offense occurs in the Church, the objective is not a single individual? **The implications go beyond the individual who was offended. For example, it affects the person's ministry and, as a result, it affects those the ministry would otherwise serve.**

Disunity dissipates the love of Christ, and offense shifts our focus from God's agenda to our agenda.

4. How does offense shift people's agendas? **They become focused on themselves, focused on what was done to them.**

5. Have you ever been offended?

    a. What were your thoughts during this time of offense?

    b. Who did you think about most?

    c. Did you focus your thoughts on God during this time?

6. Whose agenda or interests was paramount during this time, yours, or God's? **The offended; the person who was hurt**.

> Jesus knew their thoughts and said to them, "Every kingdom divided against itself will be ruined, and every city or household divided against itself will not stand.
> —Matthew 12:25 (NIV)
>
> Jesus knew their thoughts and said to them: "Any kingdom divided against itself will be ruined, and a house divided against itself will fall.
> —Luke 11:17 (NIV)

➢ *Discuss the implications of offense in local assemblies.*

7. In addition to the person against whom the wrong is done, who is affected when the brethren offend one another? (Matthew 25:40). **God/Christ is affected. Whatever we do to any of His children we do to Him.**

8. How is the local church affected when the brethren offend one another? (Matthew 12:25; Luke 11:17). **We become divided, and when divided, we cannot stand. We lose spiritual effectiveness when we're divided.**

9. What does a body of people (a local church) that cannot stand (Matthew 12:25) look like? **Ineffectiveness in the work of the ministry. No defense against the enemy. Any household torn apart by infighting will split. Success and power in the Holy Spirit rely on oneness/unit.**

> ➤ *Discuss 1 Corinthians 1:10. Ask for some characteristics of a local congregation that would indicate that the members (1) speak the same thing, (2) that there are no divisions among them, and (3) they are joined together.*

10. Whose purpose is being fulfilled when members of the body of Christ offend one another? **Satan, our adversary**.

11. If Satan can disempower just one member of us, he has in fact impaired the body. Is that a true statement? (1 Corinthians 12:12-27).

> ➤ *Discuss a practical situation in which this could happen in a local congregation.*

> *The body of Christ is intricately connected. We should be interdependent, not dependent on, or independent of one another.*

All the members of the body are interconnected and mutually dependent or supportive. No member of the body can operate at its full capacity without the cooperation and support of the other members of the body. That being the case, if one member of the body is negatively affected, then the entire body is affected. If our right arm is affected, it may not affect our digestive system or our sight. But rest assured that with a dysfunctional arm, the body will not operate at its best. The same thing applies to the spiritual body. Consequently, if one member of the body is offended, it affects the entire body by causing some level of dysfunction.

End the session with prayer. Suggested prayer points:

1. Love for the people of God; the family of God

2. Kingdom perspective that seeks out the well-being of the Church.

3. Unity in your local assembly and in the Church at large.

4. Insight to do your role in keeping the family of God together.

5. Wisdom and strength to guard your heart against offense.

6. Total eradication of offense in your local assembly.

7. Exponential growth in brotherly love, peace among the brethren, and preference for one another.

Reflection and Personal Application

Stop and think about your conduct. Have you hurt any of your brothers or sisters in Christ? Have you treated any of your brothers or sisters different from how you would like to be treated? Inversely, have you been hurt by a brother or sister in Christ? How did either situation — you hurting a brother or sister or a brother or sister hurting you — affect the ministry?

Ask God to give you such an investment in His body that the thought — let alone the act — of causing harm to any member of the body never occurs to you. Ask your Father to give you an understanding of how you or any of your brothers or sisters fit in the body. With this understanding, you will know that if one person in the body hurts, the entire body hurts, and because of your genuine interest in the well-being of the body, you will cause no harm or offense to the body. Refer to John 17:16-21 and think of what part of the body you are. Being this part of the body, if you become dysfunctional, how would that affect the body?

> The mere fact that we are all flawed in some way or another sets the stage for offense. If we live in this world, offense will come.

Session Goals

By the end of this session, participants will

- learn about emotional wounds,
- learn about character flaws, and
- learn how we all bring Matthew 18:7 to reality.

Offense Must Come

> *When two or more people interact, immediately there are differences, and this creates the perfect mix of ingredients for conflict and ultimate violation of each other.*

It is impossible to live on this earth and not hurt or be hurt by another. Why? Because people are flawed. No one is perfect, and in our imperfection, we are at risk of being hurt, and we have the propensity to hurt others.

Another thing to consider is that none of us knows of another individual who is identical to us, not only in physical appearance but in the way we think, the way we respond to people, the way we process information and experiences, the way we treat others, and the way we view ourselves. No one in the entire universe does these things in the same way as we do.

When two or more people interact, immediately there are differences, and this creates the perfect mix of ingredients for conflict and ultimate violation of each other. Therefore, unless we live in a bubble, completely isolated from people, we will encounter relational conflict. Scripture refers to this as offense. Offense must come! Matthew 18:7 validates that.

A couple of key questions to consider are (1) why do we offend one another, and (2) why do we become so hurt when we are offended? The answer to both questions is *me* or *I*. We offend others because of *me* or *I*, and we get hurt as badly as we do because of *me* or *I*.

Given that we are not insane, all of us want the best for ourselves. All of us want to avoid pain and unpleasant situations. Therefore, we naturally act in favor of the *me* or *I*, sometimes at the expense of others. This is more likely to happen when self is not crucified.

Two primary things about us make offense inevitable: character flaws and emotional wounds.

Character Flaws

A character flaw is a personal limitation or deficiency that otherwise would render the individual very functional. In general, character flaws can be categorized as minor, major, or tragic. Character flaws can be problematic to the extent that they directly affect our actions and abilities.

> *A character flaw is a personal limitation or deficiency that otherwise would render the individual very functional.*

Character flaws can be manifested in all manner of gross behaviors, such as violent temper, anger outbursts, greed, prejudice, dishonesty, and gossip, to name a few.

Alternatively, character flaws can be manifested in mostly innocuous shortcomings or personality defects that affect our motives and social interactions, such as procrastination, poor time management, misaligned values, victim mentality, perfectionism, and nit-picking.

1. What is a character flaw? **Negative qualities that affect a person's behavior.**

2. *Discuss how "minor" or "harmless" character flaws, such as procrastination or nit-picking, make us more likely to offend others.*

 **Nit-picking could cause offense or hurt to someone if the person doing the nit-picking constantly picks at or makes non-affirmative comments about a person or the person's actions. Over time, these comments could hurt the person's feelings. When taken in isolated cases, this behavior may not be a big deal, but eventually it can cause significant damage to a person's self-image.**

Procrastination could set the stage for offense to occur. For example, a person has an assignment to complete by a certain time, but he or she procrastinates and does not complete the task as required. When held accountable, the procrastinator, being defensive, lashes back instead of taking responsibility for the misconduct. The person who attempted to hold the procrastinator accountable is now offended.

Discuss the following vignette and answer the questions below.

Out of the kindness of her heart, Claudette opened her home to Carol, a sister in her church who lost her apartment because her prolonged health resulted in the loss of her job. Carol is incredibly grateful to Claudette for her generosity. Claudette has been living by herself for quite some time and is extremely neat and fussy. Everything is always in its right place. Carol is not exactly sloppy, but she is not as compulsive about being neat and clean as Claudette. Claudette makes comments, sometimes not directly to Carol, when things are not in place and squeaky clean. Sometimes Claudette openly corrects Carol when things are not done her way. Other times, Claudette anticipates Carol's behavior and comments even before she does anything. She even comments about how Carol eats. It appears as if Carol must do everything Claudette's way for her not to complain.

3. Who has the character flaw—Claudette, Carol, or both? **Claudette**

4. What is the character flaw? **Nitpicking/Faultfinding**.

5. What kind of impact can the character flaw have? Why?

   ➢ *Discuss at least two other seemingly harmless character flaws anyone could have and how they could cause offense.*

6. Identify the character flaw in the following Bible characters. Discuss if and how these character flaws caused offense then and how they could cause offense today.

   a. Naomi (Ruth 1:20-21). **Naomi was bitter. Her words could be offensive to others. "…evil man brings evil things out of the evil stored up in his heart. For the mouth speaks what the heart is full of" (Luke 6:45)**.

   b. Jacob and Rebecca (Genesis 27:16-19). **Jacob was a deceiver (in conduct and by name) and so was his mother, Rebecca. She set Jacob up to cheat his brother Esau out of his birthright and Jacob followed through with the plan. This behavior could cause conflict wherever he went**.

   c. Paul (Acts 15:36-40). **Saul was impatient with and intolerant of Mark because Mark had departed from him and Barnabas at Pamphylia and did not go with them on the mission trip. As a result, a sharp contention arose between Paul and Barnabas that led to them parting (splitting) from one another**.

> [16] She also covered his hands and the smooth part of his neck with the goatskins. [17] Then she handed to her son Jacob the tasty food and the bread she had made. [18] He went to his father and said, "My father." "Yes, my son," he answered. "Who is it?" [19] Jacob said to his father, "I am Esau your firstborn. I have done as you told me. Please sit up and eat some of my game, so that you may give me your blessing."
>
> — Genesis 27:16-19 (NIV)

Our characters are the end products of how we perceive, process, and respond to stimuli, which over time defines who we are. We all have flaws. No one is perfect. Character flaws can range from simple, harmless weaknesses to gross deficiencies.

We should note, however, that whether our flaws are minor, major, or tragic, they always interfere with our relationships. This is because our characters are who we are, and we always bring that person into our relationships

.

Emotional Wounds

> *Emotional hunger is deep-seated emotional need that drives our behavior from the subconscious.*

Emotional wounds are the result of pain inflicted on the inner person of an individual. They are damages to the self-love of a person. The result of untreated emotional wounds is emotional hunger. These are deep-seated emotional needs that drive our behavior from the subconscious.

7. *Discuss the following vignettes. Identify the emotional wound(s) in each case and discuss how the emotional wound(s) could cause offense then and in later relationships.*

Verbal Abuse: Jerome was raised in a home where his father always criticized him, and therefore he could do nothing that pleased his father. Jerome always felt as if he was not good at anything. He has met the lady he knows he wants to marry but is very unsure of himself. Now at 27, he doubts if he can be a good husband or father.

Receiving affirmation from the significant figures in our lives, especially as children, is especially important to having a sense of competence and high self-esteem; if not, we will feel insecure. A person with low self-esteem will doubt themselves and is usually very easily offended. The same is true for people who are insecure; they often are defensive and are more likely to misinterpret words and events. As a result, they offend others more easily.

People who are insecure are highly likely to compare themselves with others, and when they do, they always see themselves as less than or worse off than the other person. This all starts in the mind. The mere fact that they think to compare themselves with someone is a clear indication that they already think less of themselves.

These individuals are prone to jealousy because they tend to see others as having what they lack and desire. Often, they see others as better than they are or as having the skills and capabilities they lack or having more self-confidence or assertion than they do.

People with these emotional wounds will be hurt much more deeply than those who are aware of and are comfortable with their strengths and weaknesses. They are much more likely to feel overlooked and rejected than those who are self-confident. These individuals also are more inclined to hurt others. Feelings of jealousy can cause them to do and say things that are hurtful to those of whom they are jealous.

Insecure people also tend to be overly competitive. Without the other person knowing, they often strive to outdo the person with whom they are comparing themselves. In their efforts to outdo the next person, it is common for them to do or say offensive things to the individual, often in an effort — consciously or unconsciously — to degrade the individual. It brings an insecure person mental ease to put down a person of whom he or she is jealous.

Emotional Neglect: Sarah is now 19 years old, but during childhood, her mother was emotionally and, for the most part, physically absent from her life. She did not enjoy the love and attention every child needs and deserves from their parents.

Childhood emotional neglect creates adults who are hungry for attention. Often, it is these individuals who strive for the visible ministries and will do almost anything to get there. These individuals often do not like behind-the-scenes roles. They will do good deeds and serve diligently in ministry but with the wrong motives. Their intent usually is to capture the attention of others. This is how they feed their emotional hunger. This emotional hunger also drives individuals to seek love and attention through compromising relationships.

Controlling Parents: Lisa's parents are very controlling. They create a culture of dependence by making decisions for her. They intrude on her privacy and tell her what to do instead of engaging in discussions with her to come to cooperative decisions. Lisa feels like her opinion does not matter. Her parents say they know what is best for her. This control continued from childhood through her college years. Lisa is now 22 years old.

Those who are raised by controlling parents have an unmet need for independence and competence. These individuals doubt their own capabilities

and are poor decision makers. They are dependent on others—their friends, their spouse, their leaders, etc. Therefore, they can become burdensome in a relationship. This sets the stage for offense to occur.

> *The healing of our emotional wounds is a life-long process for most of us; hence, the church is well populated with emotionally wounded individuals.*

While it is true that those who are not members of the body of Christ have character flaws and emotional wounds, it is also true for those who are. Accepting Christ as our Lord and Savior does not miraculously heal our emotional wounds. This is a life-long process for most of us. Therefore, the Church is well populated with emotionally wounded individuals. We come with a full range of ailments that manifest in various ways, but God wants us whole.

The underlying cause for these behaviors is emotional hunger. Emotionally hungry people are simply seeking to meet their emotional needs through unhealthy means, often at other people's expense.

The emotionally wounded are more likely to feel like victims than those who are emotionally healthy. They get hurt very easily and are much more likely to be deeply hurt by almost any infraction against them. As a result, they harbor hurt that, if unaddressed, will turn into offense.

Remember, it is not so much the hurt caused by the infraction that matters. Hurt is a natural response. What really matters is how we manage the hurt. Hurt caused by an infraction against an individual with emotional wounds or emotional hunger will have a greater and more negative impact on the individual than on someone who is emotionally healthier. While none of us is completely emotionally sound, some of us are less scarred or are farther along in the healing process than others.

The emotional health of the emotionally wounded is quite frail, and they live and behave from this place of deficiency. Their conduct is directed from their subconscious, a place of hurt and brokenness.

Emotionally wounded people not only hurt more deeply, but they also handle hurt poorly. They stay hurt longer and are more likely to become offended. Because of emotional wounds, these individuals are less capable of acknowledging that infractions hurt, dealing with the hurt in a healthy manner, and seeking to break free from it. As a result, they will more likely feel offended when there is no infraction against them. They are also the ones who embellish a minor infraction and make it a bigger issue than it really is. By doing so, they feed their emotional hunger.

8. *Instruct the students to list some characteristics of the emotionally wounded. A few examples are listed below.*

a) <u>**More likely to feel like a victim than a person who is emotionally healthy**</u>.

b) <u>**Get hurt/offended very easily**</u>.

c) <u>**Much more likely to be deeply hurt by almost any infraction against them**</u>.

d) <u>**Handle hurt poorly**</u>.

e) <u>**Stay hurt longer and, as a result, are more likely to become offended**</u>.

f) <u>**Less capable of acknowledging that infractions hurt**</u>.

g) <u>**More likely feel offended when there is no infraction against them**</u>.

h) <u>**Embellish minor infractions and make them bigger issues than they really are**</u>.

i) <u>**The emotionally wounded are hurt. As stated by Bill Bowen, "Hurt people hurt people." Due to the seemingly unavoidable pain in their own lives or the impact their painful experiences have had on their lives, their response, and possible means of coping with hurt is to hurt others**</u>.

j) <u>**Project the hurt and pain they have experienced onto others**</u>.

We Are All Flawed

> *The mere fact that we are all flawed in some way sets the stage for offense. If you live in this world, offense will come.*

It is not just the emotionally wounded who cause offense. The character-flawed are likely to do so as well. As previously mentioned, all of us have some form of character flaw, and these flaws are likely to cause offense. Hurt people hurt people; no one is exempt. We all cause offense at some point in our lives. Offense must come!

Whether it is the character-flawed or the emotionally wounded, offense or hurt caused by one person to another is inevitable. Remember that the mere fact that we are all flawed in some way sets the stage for offense. Matthew 18:7 supports all of this. If you live in this world, offense will come. Now that we know that offense will come and that we will likely play a part in bringing offense to others, we need to guard our hearts so that we're not victims or perpetrators of offense.

End the session with prayer. Suggested prayer points:

1. A better understanding of yourself. Awareness of the emotional scars you carry. The grace to accept who you are.

2. A better understanding of yourself. Awareness of the character flaws you have. The grace to accept who you are.

3. Healing for childhood hurts.

4. Detachment from anything in your past that make you more likely to offend others or to be offended.

5. To become less flawed and more like Christ.

Reflection and Personal Application

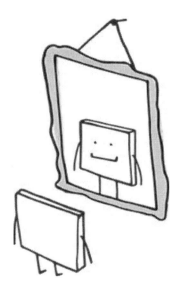

Examine your life as it is today and consider your early years to determine if any childhood experiences have left you emotionally wounded. Being emotionally wounded is nothing to be ashamed of. It is best to come to grips with the fact. Rather than deny it and limp your way through life, take it to your heavenly Father, who is your healer. He wants you whole.

In like manner, examine your life to identify your character flaws. If you find no flaws, keep looking until you find the truth about yourself. Ask the Holy Spirit to reveal the *real you* to you.

Some painful experiences may surface, but as they do, be diligent in talking to your heavenly Father, who loves you immensely and wants the absolute best for you. Write down what the Lord reveals to you, set goals for how you want to address them, and keep them in prayer before the Lord. Read scriptures that minister to the pain that surfaces. *"Beloved, I wish above all things that thou mayest prosper and be in health, even as thy soul prospereth."* (3 John 2, KJV). The health to which this passage refers is holistic health, which includes your emotional health. God wants you to be wholly healthy.

> Both Satan and God have a plan. Satan's plans toward you are evil, and God's plans toward you are good.

Session Goals

By the end of this session, participants will

- know how Satan chooses his targets,
- know what makes a person a target for Satan, and
- know that God sets boundaries and limits on Satan.

Joseph, an Example for Us

Why would God allow people to be hurt by others, especially those who are going about their business normally? Why would God allow anyone to experience the deep pain that is associated with being hurt by someone we trust? Why would this happen to someone who is seeking to do His will? One of the best answers to these questions is found in scripture in the life of Joseph, told in the book of Genesis.

Joseph was an innocent teenager, living life as he should. Whatever happened to him — being the son of his father's old age, making him his father's favorite, and receiving dreams from God that portrayed him as favorable over his brothers and his parents — were not his fault. These things happened to him, and they were the catalysts to the hurt he endured from his brothers.

One may say that he flaunted the dreams he got from God, and he might have presented himself as better than his brothers. But it should be noted that because of his immaturity, Joseph shared his dreams with his brothers and father prematurely. He was not mature enough to know that he should only share such delicate information with the "right people" and most certainly at the right time.

1. Joseph's brothers hated him for two reasons. What were they?

   a. **For being their father's favorite son. His father loved Joseph more than any of his other sons because Joseph was born to him in his old age** (Genesis 37:3-4).

   b. **For what they thought was his proud attitude of posing himself as being better than them. Joseph had two dreams: (1) that his brothers' "sheaves gathered around his and bowed down to it," indicating that he would reign over them** (Genesis 37:8), and (2) **that he would reign over his brothers and parents** (Genesis 37:9).

2. In addition to hate, what other emotion did Joseph's brothers have toward him? **Jealousy** (Genesis 37:10).

3. How did Joseph's brothers act on their hate for him? **They sold him to the Ishmaelites** (Genesis 37:27).

4. As a result of being sold by his brothers, what other painful experiences did Joseph endure?

   a. **Accused of rape by Potiphar's wife** (Genesis 39:6-18)

   b. **False imprisonment** (Genesis 39:20)

Note that Joseph was innocent in all of this. He had not done any harm to his brothers, and he did not rape Potiphar's wife.

5. Discuss how God navigated everything that happened to Joseph to work out His plan.

   a. **Thrown in a pit instead of being killed by his brothers**.

   b. **Sold to the Ishmaelites**.

   c. **Sold to Potiphar**.

   d. **Thrown in jail where he then had the opportunity to interpret a dream for one of Pharaoh's butler and baker**.

   e. **Interpreted Pharoah's dream and advised Pharaoh on how he could address the problem the dream predicted**.

> [3] Now Israel loved Joseph more than any of his other sons, because he had been born to him in his old age; and he made an ornate robe for him. [4] When his brothers saw that their father loved him more than any of them, they hated him and could not speak a kind word to him. [8] His brothers said to him, "Do you intend to reign over us? Will you actually rule us?" And they hated him all the more because of his dream and what he had said. [9] Then he had another dream, and he told it to his brothers. "Listen," he said, "I had another dream, and this time the sun and moon and eleven stars were bowing down to me." [10] When he told his father as well as his brothers, his father rebuked him and said, "What is this dream you had? Will your mother and I and your brothers actually come and bow down to the ground before you?"
>
> —Genesis 37:3-4, 8-10

f. **Pharaoh discerned Joseph's wisdom; put him in charge of all the lands of Egypt**.

6. What was God's ultimate plan? (Genesis 41:57) **Joseph was used to save the lives of many. During the famine, people, including Joseph's brothers came from all countries to buy grain from Joseph**.

> And all countries came into Egypt to Joseph for to buy corn; because that the famine was so sore in all lands.
> —Genesis 41:57 (KJV)
>
> And the Lord was with Joseph, and he was a prosperous man; and he was in the house of his master the Egyptian.
> —Genesis 39:2 (NIV)

Joseph's brothers had a plan, but God had a plan that was well beyond theirs. Note that in all the injustice Joseph endured, the favor of God was upon him. The Lord was with him. His ways pleased the Lord. Read Genesis 39:2.

7. Forgiveness goes both ways. We should be able to give and receive forgiveness. What evidence is there that Joseph's brothers did not readily receive forgiveness from their brother Joseph? Read Genesis 43:15-31; 45:3-14; 50:15-20. **Even after all that Joseph did to show them that he had forgiven them, they feared that he would take revenge after their father died.**

8. God has a plan for your life as well. Identify some lessons learned from Joseph's conduct that, if employed in your life, would make room for God's plan in your life also.

a. **Joseph's ways pleased the Lord**.

b. **Nowhere in the Scriptures do we see Joseph complaining or trying to justify himself**.

c. **Joseph did not retaliate**.

d. **Joseph never deterred from a faithful walk with God**.

e. **Joseph forgave his brothers**.

By the time all this happened, it had been over ten years since the brothers had seen Joseph. When they came to Egypt to purchase grain, God would have it that Joseph recognized them, but they did not recognize him. As predicted by Joseph's dreams, the brothers all bowed to him because he was an important person, but even more so because it was in God's plan.

Joseph's brothers were at his mercy. They were subject to him. He could have ordered, plotted, or planned for any measure of evil to be done to them in revenge, but that would have aborted God's plan. After Joseph revealed himself to his brothers, of course they were afraid. They knew that Joseph had the power to do whatever he wanted to do to them. But remember, Joseph's ways were pleasing to God. He chose not to take revenge but to stay in the will of God. He revealed to them that God meant for good what they meant for evil (Genesis 50:20). They thought they were getting rid of him, but he was sent there to save their lives, in particular the tribes of Israel. God had a plan!

Our experience may not be as extreme as Joseph's. No one may have threatened to kill us, throw us in a well, or sell us to merchants. No one may have accused us of attempted rape or put us in jail for something we did not do. But it is highly likely that we have been hurt by those we love and trust and at a time when we least expected it. As in Joseph's case, so it is with us. God has a plan through all the events of our lives. We are simply conduits for His plan.

Both Satan and God Have a Plan

While the intent of these negative actions toward us is to hurt us, God's intent is to turn them into good.

9. Can you think of a hurtful experience you have had through which God worked for your good and the good of others?
    a. Did you know at the onset or while going through the situation that God had a bigger plan?

    b. How did you first feel about the situation?

    c. Did you try to justify yourself?

    d. Did you retaliate?

    e. Was God's plan accomplished? If not, what hindered His plan? If so, what facilitated His plan?

    f. Did your ways please the Lord throughout the process?

> *God always has a bigger and better plan than we can ever conceive. The key thing to note is that God's plans not only work for our good, but they also always work for the benefit of others.*

At times God allows Satan's plans, which sometimes are hurt caused by those we love and trust, so that He can work out His bigger plan for us and for others. God always has a bigger and better plan than we can ever conceive. The key thing to note is that God's plans not only work for our good, but they also always work for the benefit of others.

It's interesting to note that both Satan and God have a plan. Satan's plan toward us is evil, and God's plan toward us is good. However, although Satan hates everyone, for he has no love in him, he specifically targets those who are clearly living a life in opposition to his principles. He does not waste his resources on those who are straddling the fence between God and him. Even if you are passively enlisted in his army, he already has you. His work concerning you is already done.

Also note that in his efforts to enlarge his army, he does not go after just anyone in God's army. His focus is those who are making a difference in the body of Christ. He attacks those who allow God to use them, those with tapped or untapped potential, those who are tearing down his strongholds, those who own and are pursuing the promises of God.

Are You a Target?

Job was a target (Job 1:1-12).

Satan had been roaming the earth, surveying his domain (Job 1:6-7; 1 John 5:19; Revelation 12:9), but he came up empty. Job's troubles began when God presented him to Satan as a shining example of virtue. *"Have you considered my servant Job?"* God asks Satan. *"There is no one on earth like him; he is blameless and upright, a man who fears God and shuns evil"* (Job 1:8, NIV).

God allowed Satan to afflict Job. This was not punishment for Job. God himself said Job was "blameless and upright." Job suffered because his life was pleasing to God, not because he was out of fellowship with God.

Satan did not agree with God's view of Job's good character. Instead, he inferred that Job had a selfish motive, a cynical reason for obeying and trusting God (Job 1:9-22). *"Does Job fear God for nothing?"* Satan asks. Satan insinuates that Job is simply devoted to God because God has blessed him with material things. He implies that Job is a fair-weather friend. *"Have you not put a hedge around him and his household and everything he has?"* Satan argues. *"You have blessed the work of his hands, so that his flocks and herds are spread throughout the land"* (Job 1:10, NIV). But God knew Job way better than Satan did.

Satan challenges God that if He takes away Job's many blessings, God will find that Job is no friend of His. *"Stretch out your hand and strike everything he has,"* Satan dares God, *"and he will surely curse you to your face"* (Job 2:5, NIV). But Satan is proven wrong. After a series of terrible tragedies strike Job, he tears his robe and shaves his head. He falls to the ground in worship, saying, *"The Lord gave and the Lord has taken away; may the name of the Lord be praised." In all this, Job did not sin by charging God with wrongdoing"* (Job 1:21b-22, NIV).

10. Why was Job a target? **Because he was blameless and upright. He was a man who feared God and rejected evil** (Job 1:8).

11. Under what circumstance was Satan able to attack Job? **Only when God gave him permission** (Job 1:12).

12. What was Satan's objective? **To prove Job a liar. To defy Job's confession of faith to God** (Job 1:9-11).

13. Can you think of a time when you were a target? Why were you a target?

> *When we are not in an offensive position against Satan, he knows that it is quite easy for him to fully lure us on his side.*

Those of us who have been in the church know very well that there are folks in the church who are not a threat to the devil. The devil knows that in many ways, he already has them; therefore, he has no need to target them. The fact that they are not actively and openly opposing him is a clear message that they are not people who operate on the offense.

If people do not see the need to live their lives in an offensive position against Satan, then it is quite easy for Satan to catch them off guard. If you claim to be walking with the Lord and have not been attacked by the devil, take a close assessment of your relationship with Christ. Ask yourself, "Am I truly related to Christ or to the devil?"

Remember, the devil only targets those he knows are not devoted to him but are devoted to God. If he knows he already has you, there is no need to try to deter you. If you are a saint who is sold out for Jesus — and Jesus alone — and you have not yet been seriously attacked by the devil, watch out, and be careful not to be ignorant of Satan's devices because if you are, he could get the better of you. Ask yourself these questions: Can "God present me to be tempted?" "Do I meet the criteria to be presented to Satan to be tempted?"

End the session with prayer. Suggested prayer points:

1. Grace to allow the hand (will) of God in your life under all circumstances, even in difficult circumstances.

2. To live a life that always pleases God, even under difficult circumstances.

3. The favor of God upon your life.

4. The same for others in your class/group and for the members of your local church.

Reflection and Personal Application

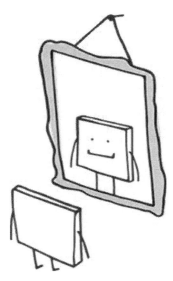

Consider these two questions: "Can God present me to be tempted?" and "Am I living a life that gives God the assurance that because of my connection to Him I can stand the tests of life?"

Understand that you will be under the attack of the enemy when you are in right standing with God. The day God considers you upright, the day you give Him the assurance that your devotion to Him is uncompromising, you will become a candidate for presentation to Satan by God to be tempted.

Examine your life to determine if there is anything you are doing or if you have a mind-set that compromises your devotion to God. Do a true introspection and be honest with yourself. Do you walk uprightly? Do you truly abjure evil?

As the Holy Spirit reveals the answers to these questions, write them down so that you can be reminded of the changes you need to make to improve the areas in which spiritual growth and maturity are needed. Make these your prayer points for further spiritual growth. Use scripture references as needed.

Unfortunately, when we are hurt by others, most of us harbor the hurt long enough for it to cause us spiritual and emotional damage. An infraction against us from any source will cause hurt. So, it is natural to hurt. But when we harbor hurt, it leads to offense, and that opens the door to spiritual death, making the strategy of the enemy successful.

Session Goals

By the end of this session, participants will

- know how to best handle hurt,
- understand the process, from the initial infraction to bitterness, and
- learn how hurt differs from unforgiveness.

Hurt Is Okay

If you live on this earth, someone will offend you. Offense is accompanied by hurt and pain; therefore, at some point in life, we all will experience hurt to some degree. Hurt is a part of the journey of life. It is totally okay to feel hurt. Do not deny or suppress your feelings. Hurt is a natural response to a painful encounter.

After having a painful experience with another individual, hurt could be an integral step on your path toward healing. But it could also be the very thing that stagnates you.

1. A natural and common response to offense is hurt. Why? **It's an emotional response. It's a defense mechanism, but not all defense mechanisms are healthy. Hurt is a natural response of a person who has been wronged.**

A defense mechanism is a coping technique that reduces anxiety arising from unacceptable or potentially harmful impulses.

Britannica.com / Human Psychology

2. Hurt can be considered a defense mechanism. What is a defense mechanism? **An unconscious coping strategy used to deal with conflict and problems in life.**

Note that it is possible to be hurt and not be aware of it. That is when it becomes a defense mechanism. This is more likely to occur in the Church because the unspoken expectation is that we should always be happy. We should not hurt when bad things happen. We should smile our way through it, even when we are dying on the inside.

Because of this notion in the Church, hurt is often misunderstood and misguided. As such, many of our brothers and sisters in Christ suppress their hurt. Some suppress their hurt so far into their subconscious that they become unaware of their inner brokenness. This is when hurt becomes a defense mechanism.

3. Which comes first, offense — the wrong deed done to you — or hurt? **The wrong deed / the infraction**.

4. What might hurt look like when one is offended? Try to think of positive attributes associated with hurt. **Passive aggression, withdrawal, critical, uncooperative/contrary, insulting, vindictive, offensive to others, etc. I cannot think of any positive attributes associated with hurt. So, I would say that although hurt is a natural response to an infraction against us, it is not good for us. If something isn't good for us, we want to get rid of it as quickly as possible.**

5. Because of the hypocrisy and possibly lack of knowledge, fellow believers in Christ — leaders and parishioners alike — often misjudge hurt for **unforgiveness**. This is very wrong and is a huge mistake.

➢ *Discuss the following vignettes. At what stage do you think these characters are hurt or offended (in a state of unforgiveness) and why?*

Sister ABC is single and without children. She has been a member of XYZ Global Ministries for the past 17 years. She has served in the ministry faithfully and sacrificially. She is a faithful tither and is quite charitable to the ministry. Unexpectedly she had a fall in her house that made her unable to work. She, for as long as she could, has used her savings to pay her bills and purchase groceries. She has now expired all her savings and has no option but to ask for help. Her first thought was to ask her church. "That's what the church is for.," she thought. Upon posing the request to her church, she was required to fill out several forms, she felt as if she were applying for a loan. The committee reviewed the forms and denied her "application," indicating she had not exhausted all her options. For example, there are community agencies that could help her, that she had not approached. Sister ABC was shocked and grossly disappointed with the response, but by the grace of God, her needs were met. The God she serves did not fail her. After getting the response from her church, she opted to visit the church closest to her home for about a month before returning to her home church. Upon returning to her church, she slowly got back to her duties in the ministry and has been serving faithfully since then.

Does Sister ABC's reaction to the response from the church indicate that she was unforgiving or that she was hurt? Why? At what point in her response was she hurt? At what point was she offended (unforgiving)?

What emotions do you think Sister ABC was feeling?

Samantha is in Bible study and the topic is wholeness, emotional healing. This is a small group that has been meeting for several years, so the members know each other very well and everyone feels it is a safe place to share and be transparent. The scripture being discussed is Luke 8:43-48, the woman with the issue of blood. Samantha saw this as an opportunity to obtain healing for a long-standing, deep-seated emotional wound with which she had been living. So, she shared that at the age of 8, her father started sexually molesting her and that it continued into her mid-teen years. She cried uncontrollably as she shared her story and expressed how badly that experience has impacted her life, even her marriage. She further shared that her father was never held responsible for what he did to her, and even more painful, her grandmother knew what was happening, and did nothing about it. Instead of the group counseling and giving Samantha comfort and guidance, the general message she got from them was she must forgive, she cannot allow what happened to her affect her that way, she should forget about what happened and live her life, especially since it happened so long ago. They even implied that Christians should not carry those memories. Samantha was shocked at their response and was left confused because she thought by sharing it, she would get the help she needed. She continued to attend the studies, but from then on, she mainly listened. Even if she had something to share, she refrained from doing so, because she was unsure of the response she would get.

- *Who, if anyone, in this vignette is unforgiving? Why?*
- *Do you think Samantha is unforgiving, hurt, or both hurt and unforgiving?*
- *What do you think the members of the group think about Samantha – she is hurt, unforgiving, or both? Why?*

6.   Offense in any context is hurtful, but it is most detrimental when it occurs in the body of Christ. Why do you think offense that takes place in the Church is most hurtful? (Read Psalm 55:12-14.)

> [12] If an enemy were insulting me, I could endure it; if a foe were rising against me, I could hide. [13] But it is you, a man like myself, my companion, my close friend, [14] with whom I once enjoyed sweet fellowship at the house of God, as we walked about among the worshipers.
> —Psalm 55:12-14 (NIV)

a.   **Our brothers and sisters in Christ are people with whom we enjoy sweet fellowship at the house of God.**

b.   **We worship with our brothers and sisters in Christ.**

c.   **The Church becomes our family, especially those in the local assembly in which we worship.**

d.   **The Scriptures speak in many places in the Bible about loving one another, so, as believers we ought to love one another.**

e.   **The church should be a place of refuge and healing, not a place where we get damaged.**

f.   **We can expect to be offended by our enemies and those outside the Body of Christ but not our brethren.**

It is not surprising — and therefore much less devastating — when a person who is not under the lordship of Christ hurts us compared to when a fellow brother or sister in Christ does. As David points out, these are people with whom we worship. They are people who call on the same God we call on. We attend prayer meetings with them, sing in the choir with them, enjoy praise and worship that they lead, go on mission trips with them, take communion/Lord's Supper with them, sit under their preaching and teaching, and might have even had them lay hands on us and pray.

> ➤ *It is said that "blood is thicker than water." Compare offense caused by family members (saved and unsaved) to those caused by fellow brothers and sisters in Christ. Discuss the impact of both circumstances on the offended and on others.*

7.   The hurt we feel from church hurt can sometimes be unclear to the one that is hurt and to others. A few misconceptions that can emerge are:

a.   **Difficulty separating the actions from the person who commit the act.**

b.   **Difficulty understanding how such pain could come out of the Church and from one of His own against one of His own.**

c.   **Difficulty disentangling mixed feelings about God's love.**

8.   If it is okay to hurt, does it ever become not okay to hurt? If so, when? **Although it is okay to hurt, it is not okay to stop at the hurt. It is not okay to linger in the hurt. Hurt should be a response to the painful encounter, not the result or outcome of the encounter. When we are wounded and broken, we cannot be of much use to God. We must be restored to health before God can use us.**

> *Offense (infractions) will come if we interact with other people. It is our response to the infraction that matters.*

Hurt is the first response to an interpersonal infraction, or what the scripture refers to as offense in Matthew 18:7. Naturally, the infraction is followed by hurt. If the hurt is not addressed in a healthy and timely manner, it could lead to offense that, and if not addressed, could lead to bitterness. Refer to figure 1 on page 4.

Offense can take place in any context: our families, friendships, our place of employment, or in any situation that involves another person. Offenses that occur outside the Church may not be as devastating as those that occur in the Church, but either way, we are still distracted from our calling.

> Woe unto the world because of offences! for it must needs be that offences come; but woe to that man by whom the offence cometh!
> —Matthew 18:7 (KJV)

Despite the source or context of the infraction, the hurt that results from it is not the problem. Offense or infractions will come if we interact with other people. It is our response to the infraction that matters.

Unfortunately, when offense comes our way, most of us get hurt and harbor the hurt long enough for it to cause us spiritual and emotional damage. While it is natural to hurt, harboring the hurt is unhealthy; it leads to offense, and that opens the door to spiritual death, making the strategy of the enemy successful. See figure 3 on page 4.

9.   Unaddressed hurt will go from healthy hurt to damaging, toxic hurt. So how do we address the hurt?

    a.   **Acknowledge that you hurt. Do not deny it.**

    b.   **Run to God, the one true healer.**

    c.   **Encourage yourself.**

  d.   **Do not blame the Church. Do not blame God.**

  e.   **Prioritize your own emotional recovery. Take care of yourself.**

➤ *Discuss 1 Samuel 30:1-6.*

And it came to pass, when David and his men were come to Ziklag on the third day, that the Amalekites had invaded the south, and Ziklag, and smitten Ziklag, and burned it with fire; ² And had taken the women captives, that were therein: they slew not any, either great or small, but carried them away, and went on their way. ³ So David and his men came to the city, and, behold, it was burned with fire; and their wives, and their sons, and their daughters, were taken captives. ⁴ Then David and the people that were with him lifted up their voice and wept, until they had no more power to weep. ⁵ And David's two wives were taken captives, Ahinoam the Jezreelitess, and Abigail the wife of Nabal the Carmelite. ⁶ And David was greatly distressed; for the people spake of stoning him, because the soul of all the people was grieved, every man for his sons and for his daughters: but David encouraged himself in the Lord his God.

—1 Samuel 30:1-6, NIV

10.　What wrong if any was done to David? **His own brethren blamed him for the loss and threatened to kill him.**

11.　Why did David need to encourage himself? **No one was on his side. He had no one to turn to.**

12.　What kind of emotions do you think David was feeling? Do you think David was hurt? Do you think he was offended? Refer to figure 2 on page 4. **David might have been hurt because he had to encourage himself. I see no evidence that he was offended.**

If you are struggling with pain due to interpersonal infractions, please know you are not alone. You are still in the center of the loving Father's love.

End the session with prayer. Suggested prayer points:

1. Grace and strength to deal with hurt in a healthy and timely manner.

2. Faith and trust in your heavenly Father to allow Him to heal your heart of hurt.

3. Emotional healing for your family, your local church, and for the body of Christ.

4. Healing for broken relationships and families in your church.

Reflection and Personal Application

Read and meditate upon 2 Corinthians 2:11. Try to identify and write down the terms on which Satan seems to get the better of you to cause you to hurt most deeply. Write down what you can do differently to be victorious in the areas in which Satan seems to get the better of you most times.

Ask God to give you the grace to handle hurt in a timely and healthy manner. Ask Him to help you not to cause hurt to others while you are hurting. Ask Him to teach you what handling hurt in a healthy manner looks like.

> Forgiveness is a mandate. It is a dictate, a command, a directive, an order. It is not a request. It is not negotiable.

Session Goals

By the end of this session, participants will

- understand that the God-given mandate to forgive demands a "Yes",
- be informed or reminded of what God has said in His Word about forgiveness, and
- realize that God has already provided everything we need to help us forgive.

Our Free Will Can Be a Snare

The first most absolute truth about forgiveness that we must embrace is that it is a mandate. When a person requests something of us, we can respond with "Yes" or "No" and the person making the request expects either of the two responses. By the mere fact that a request was made, it is apparent to the person who made the request and to the respondent that a "Yes" or "No" is quite acceptable. We can even respond to a request with "I don't know," "Wait a minute," or "Maybe" and that would be acceptable as well.

But although we have volition to say "Yes" or "No" to a command, saying "No," given that it's coming from a trusted source and one with authority, is often to our disadvantage. We are expected to say "Yes" to a command but are not forced to do so. Our response to a command should be definite; it should be "Yes" or "No." Responding with "I don't know," "Wait a minute," or "Maybe" is not acceptable.

God Himself gives us the command to forgive. It comes directly from the Word of God, and God expects complete obedience to His Word, especially if we say we love Him. John 14:15 (NIV) says. "*If ye love me, keep my commandments.*" Therefore, according to scripture, the absolute best way to demonstrate our love for God is to obey Him, period.

God wants complete, non-negotiated, unmitigated obedience in every area of our lives, even when it hurts. You can do it. He has not asked anything of you for which His grace is not sufficient. You must not let your free will become a snare.

1. We have a mandate. What is a mandate?
   a. **A dictate**
   b. **A command**
   c. **A directive**
   d. **An order**
   e. **It is not a request.**
   f. **It is not negotiable**

2. When we disobey a command, we will face **consequences**.

3. According to John 14:15, What is the best way to show our love for God? **Obey Him**. Jesus is our example of obedience. Read Luke 22:42-43.

4. While acknowledging the bitterness of the cup before Him, Jesus **obeyed** His Father all the way to the cross of calvary.

5. At what point did an angel come to strengthen Jesus. **When He surrendered His will to the Father. He said, "not my will, but thine, be done."**

> [42] Saying, Father, if thou be willing, remove this cup from me: nevertheless not my will, but thine, be done. [43] And there appeared an angel unto him from heaven, strengthening him.
> —Luke 22:42-43 (KJV)
>
> If ye love me, keep my commandments.
> —John 14:15 (KJV)

6. What does Jesus' experience tell you?
   If I surrender my will, God will send me help/strength to obey Him / to forgive as He has commanded.

7. What assurance is there in 2 Corinthians 12:9 that you can forgive? **God's grace is enough to enable me to forgive. When I'm weak, He gives me the strength to forgive.**

We Cannot Argue with Scripture

These scriptures highlight the fact that forgiveness is indeed a mandate, not a request. Identify what each scripture reference says about forgiveness.

8. Colossians 3:13

   a. **Bear with each other if there is a conflict**.
   b. **Forgive as the Lord forgave you**.
9. Ephesians 4:31-32
   a. **Get rid of all bitterness, rage, and anger; brawling; and slander, along with every form of malice**.
   b. **Be kind and compassionate to one another**.
   c. **Forgive each other, just as in Christ God forgave you**.

The Greek word for ought is deh-on. It means necessary, behoove, must (needs be), or need. This is an expectation placed upon us by God. It provides no wiggle room, no matter what.

10.   Matthew 18:21-22— **We should forgive our brothers and sisters who sin against us, not seven times but seventy times seven**.

11.   2 Corinthians 2:5-8

a.   **Forgive anyone who has caused grief and comfort him, so that he will not be overwhelmed by excessive sorrow.**

b.   **Reaffirm your love for your offender**.

c.   **Forgive and comfort your offender**.

12.   Mark 11:25-26— **Forgive your offender, so that your Father in heaven may forgive you of your sins**.

13.   Discuss what the word *"that"* means in Mark 11:25.

14.   Matthew 6:14-15— **If we forgive our offenders, God will forgive us. If we do not forgive, God will not forgive us of our sins.**

15.   Psalm 66:18— **God will not hear us or forgive us of our sins if we have ill feelings toward others**.

16. Luke 6:37— **Forgive, and you will be forgiven**.

We are to forgive, just as God forgave us. It is a command.

17. Can you think of any situation that is so bad that it's acceptable not to forgive the offender? Are there any exceptions to the rule? Why? Why not?

18. What evidence is there that God has not asked anything of us that He has not done or is not doing? Refer to John 3:16, 1 John 1:9, Hebrews 7:25, and Romans 5:8.

a.   John 3:16— **God gave His only begotten son through an ignominious death to redeem humankind back to Him**.

b.   1 John 1:9— **If we confess our sins to God, He is faithful and just. He will forgive us of our sins and will purify us from all unrighteousness**.

c.   Hebrews 7:25— **Christ now lives to make intercession for us**.

d.   Romans 5:8— **While we were sinners, before we asked for forgiveness, Christ died for our sins**.

[21] Then came Peter to him, and said, Lord, how oft shall my brother sin against me, and I forgive him? till seven times? [22] Jesus saith unto him, I say not unto thee, Until seven times: but, Until seventy times seven.
—Matthew 18:21-22 (KJV)

And when ye stand praying, forgive, if ye have ought against any: that your Father also which is in heaven may forgive you your trespasses.
—Mark 11:25 (KJV)

We are told in Matthew 18:21-22 that our acts of forgiveness toward our brothers and sisters should be unlimited. God demands unlimited forgiveness from us, not conditional forgiveness, and certainly not the "three strikes and you're out" or the "once bitten, twice shy." Attitude. Think! What if God took that position toward us? His mercies are from everlasting to everlasting (Psalm 103:17; 100:5). And He has commanded us to forgive others as He has forgiven us — repeatedly. It's a mandate! Do not let your free will to choose become a snare. Say yes!

> 25 And when you stand praying, if you hold anything against anyone, forgive them, so that your Father in heaven may forgive you your sins." 26 But if you do not forgive, neither will your father which is in heaven forgive your trespasses.
> —Mark 11:25-26 (KJV)

End the session with prayer. Suggested prayer points:

1. A heart of total obedience to the Word of God. The will to choose to obey God.

2. Pure love for God, demonstrated by total obedience to Him.

3. Eradication of everything that challenges your ability to fully obey God's Word.

4. A heart of compassion; a forgiving heart.

5. Love for your enemy.

6. The grace to speak well of those who speak evil of you.

Reflection and Personal Application

Do you find it difficult to forgive? If so, think carefully, and try to identify why you find it difficult, especially seeing you now know or have been reminded of the detrimental consequences of unforgiveness. Be honest with yourself as you do this introspection. This is between you and your heavenly Father. Ask Him to show you your inward parts. There may be suppressed issues that have hardened your heart to your offenders. Only the Holy Spirit can make you aware of these things.

As the Holy Spirit reveals these things to you, write them down and pray diligently over them until you see changes. Read scripture passages that address these issues as well. It is by the washing of the Word that you will be cleansed (Ephesians 5:26).

> A half-truth is a lie, but it's even more dangerous than a full lie. A lie you can detect at some stage, but a half-truth is sure to mislead you for long.

Session Goals

By the end of this session, participants will

- understand what gives Satan the opening to lie to them,
- know the results of Satan's lies to them, and
- know what they can do to combat Satan's lies.

It's A Lie

The offended must not believe the lies of the enemy that they are responsible for what has happened, especially if it is a child who has been victimized by an adult. This is another trick of the enemy.

Satan in his shrewdness, seeks to make the biggest impact possible when he strikes.

Therefore, not only does he seek to ruin the offended by snaring them with unforgiveness toward the offender, but he also does so by accusing them, making them blame themselves, which often, depending on the circumstance, result in negative emotions.

1. What are some examples of negative emotions that result from self-blame?
   a. **Regret**
   b. **Shame**
   c. **Guilt**

Are regret, shame, and guilt synonyms? They feel very similar, and they are all unpleasant. There is an instinct to want to hide or cover up when one feels this way. Frequently we

are embarrassed to admit or talk about these emotions with others. There is a sense of being dirty, damaged, or less than when we feel this way. Sometimes we tend to believe that these emotions define us (at least to some degree). This is what Satan wants, that is why he lies to us.

These feelings are often triggered by similar types of events; all negative. It could be the memories of negative experiences. These memories are sometimes hard to let go, and they open doors for Satan to lie to us.

It is human nature to silently relive things; to think about things repeatedly, especially things that are unresolved. Without deliberate efforts being taken to stop this unhealthy thought pattern, it will be an unbroken destructive cycle. The more you think about that painful, or the unresolved issue, the more the devil can lie to you about what happened, why it happened, and who is responsible. This can occur in childhood and in adulthood.

2. What is the difference between regret, shame, and guilt?

 Note that these emotions are unique in that they all apply to the past, so it can get overwhelming when a person thinks about the prospect of never being able to undo whatever has led them to feel this way. The feelings of helplessness brought on by the fact that nothing can change the past worsens regret, shame, and guilt.

a. Regret traps you in the **past**. It forces you to **relive** the past with sadness and **disappointment**.

b. Shame is closely tied to **pain** and is also the result of a false sense of **condemnation**. It is the painful feeling arising from **remembering** something **hurtful** that was done to you, for example, sexual molestation, domestic violence, verbal abuse, or insults.

Shame is incredibly unhealthy because it lowers one's self-esteem, causing feelings of unworthiness, and behaviors that reinforce that negative self-image.

> *Shame is a painful feeling about how we appear to others (and to ourselves) and does not necessarily depend on our having done anything.*

c. Guilt is **condemnation**. In this case, because it is due to a **lie** from the **enemy**, guilt is illegitimate condemnation. It is undue or unwarranted **responsibility** for wrongdoing. Guilt surrounds or is linked to an event and does not define the person.

3. The more you **rehearse** the incident in your **mind** the greater the chance you will feel **regret**, shame, or guilt.

4. The devil cannot read your **mind**, but your **words** and **actions** tell him where you are emotionally and mentally. First, you start with the **thoughts** about what happened, your thoughts progress to **words**, and your words then lead to **actions**.

➤ *Discuss the following vignettes.*

Mary is in a tumultuous marriage. Her husband works long hours. He is experiencing a lot of stress due to his job, so when he comes home, he expects peace and quietness. Recently, after the birth of their twins, the husband has obviously become angry at the state of their home and the wife's preoccupation with the children and has hit her on several occasions. The husband, after physically assaulting his wife, tells her that it is her fault that he hits her because she gives more attention to the twins than to him or to her housekeeping responsibilities and she believes him. Now she blames herself because her marriage is spiraling out of control and if she were a good wife, it would not have happened.

- *What is Mary experiencing, guilt, shame, or regret? Why?*
- *What got her to experience this emotion?*
- *Is this emotion warranted?*
- *What can she do to stop this flood of emotion?*
- *What are some possible outcomes if she continues to feel this way?*

Samantha was sexually molested by her father from age 8 until her mid-teen years. She cannot stop thinking about what happened to her. She is now married and in her mid-thirties, but she thinks about what happened to her practically every day. She is married, but she feels ugly, damaged, and sometimes dirty. She does not feel like she deserves a husband. She often dresses overly modestly because she does not feel pretty and, in some way, she feels that would ward off any other sexual predator from her.

- *What is Samantha experiencing, guilt, shame, or regret? Why?*
- *What got her to having this emotion?*
- *Is this emotion warranted?*
- *What can she do to stop this flood of emotion?*
- *What are some possible outcomes if she continues to feel this way?*

Tracy got into one of the most intense arguments with her twin sister about her mother's will after her mother passed. They both said some very unkind things to each other. After Tracy felt she unloaded all the venom she thought she had for her sister, she slammed the door, and got in her car and left. The relationship is now very awkward, but neither of them is making the effort to make amends. However, Tracy feels bad on the inside, but she is too stubborn to admit it. Not a waking moment goes by, and she does not think about what she could have done or said that could have prevented such a heated argument and now, the malice between her and her twin sister.

- *What is Tracy experiencing, guilt, shame, or regret? Why?*
- *What got her to having this emotion?*
- *What can she do to stop this flood of emotion?*

5. Satan is what?
   a. Revelation 12:10. **Accuser of the brethren.**
   b. John 8:44. **A liar.**
   c. Matthew 4:3. **The tempter.**

Combatting Satan's Lies

Jesus showed us how we can defend ourselves by planting our roots in His word and surrendering to the Holy Spirit. Because of His truth, we can see the lies Satan places before us — when Satan tells us a lie, we can turn to the Holy Spirit and Scripture and see what they say. For example, when Satan tells us that we are not loved or are unlovable, we can turn to scripture and see how deeply our heavenly Father loves us. Just as Jesus relied on the Spirit and Scripture to defeat Satan, so can we.

> And I heard a loud voice saying in heaven, Now is come salvation, and strength, and the kingdom of our God, and the power of his Christ: for the accuser of our brethren is cast down, which accused them before our God day and night.
> —Revelation 12:10 (KJV)
>
> Ye are of your father the devil, and the lusts of your father ye will do. He was a murderer from the beginning, and abode not in the truth, because there is no truth in him. When he speaketh a lie, he speaketh of his own: for he is a liar, and the father of it.
> —John 8:44 (KJV)
>
> And when the tempter came to him, he said, If thou be the Son of God, command that these stones be made bread.
> —Matthew 4:3 (KJV)

End the session with prayer. Suggested prayer points:

1.   A healthy thought life — to think upon things that are positive, truth, good report, pure, lovely, admirable, and praiseworthy.

2.   High sensitivity to the lies of the devil; that you will readily recognize his lies.

3.   An awakening of the authority in you to use the Word of God against the enemy when he tries to lie to you.

4.   To lay down and leave any feelings of guilt, shame, or regret that you have at Jesus' feet.

Reflection and Personal Application

Read Philippians 4:8 in at least three versions of the Bible.

Write down:

– one *truth* about you that is in God's Word on which you can think.

– one *pure* (genuine or unadulterated) thing about you on which you can think.

– one *lovely* (pleasant) thing about you on which you can think.

– one *good* thing about you on which you can think.

– one *virtuous* (honest) thing about you on which you can think.

– one *praise-worthy* thing about you on which you can think.

> The self is who you are, not what you do or say. The self is the real you; it is the inner you. It drives what you think, desire, say, and do.

Session Goals

By the end of this session, participants will

- be more keenly aware of existing spiritual contaminants, particularly those that are not visible to the naked eye, and
- recognize their greatest enemy or challenge to a triumphant Christian life and what needs to be done to conquer it.

Spiritual Termites

Unforgiveness is likened to a spiritual termite. There are many other spiritual termites in the church, such as jealousy, pride, envy, ingratitude, competition, and self-doubt. Because of the nature of these spiritual termites, they are at epidemic rates. Termites feed on wooden structures such as trees, buildings, and furniture and can go undetected for a long time. It is often when the strength of the structure is tested or needed that it is discovered that it is weak because termites have been eating away at it. A structure that is infested with termites can be hollow on the inside but look quite fine on the outside.

Spiritual termites can go undetected to the natural eyes for an awfully long time. This is unfortunate, but these spiritual termites are very prevalent in the church because the gift of discernment of spirits is not operating in the church as it should be.

Christians that house spiritual termites can continue to operate in their roles as if all is well. They could be doing anything in ministry — preaching, teaching, singing in the choir, ushering, maintaining the church building, cleaning the churchyard, or visiting the sick. Like the wooden structures that house termites, these Christians look fine from the outside until a storm comes or until pressure is applied. Then it becomes apparent that their strength is gone.

What spiritual termite(s) did the following Bible characters have?

1. Saul: **jealousy, insecurity, self-doubt** (1 Samuel 18:6-12).

    2.   Cain: **jealousy** (Genesis 4:3-5, 8).

    3.   Jacob: **trickery, dishonesty** (Genesis 27:18-27).

    4.   Esau: **imprudence/carelessness, impulsiveness** (Genesis 25:27-32).

5. The unmerciful servant: **unforgiveness, greed** (Matthew 18:28-29).

6. Judas: **disloyalty, greed** (Luke 22:3-6, 47-48).

7. Haman: **hate, pride, prejudice** (Esther 3:5-6).

8. The rich young ruler: **materialism, displaced affection, religiosity** (Matthew 19:16-24, Mark 10:17-22).

9. Miriam and Aaron: **jealousy, pride** (Numbers 12:1-3).

> [28] But when that servant went out, he found one of his fellow servants who owed him a hundred silver coins. He grabbed him and began to choke him. 'Pay back what you owe me!' he demanded. [29] "His fellow servant fell to his knees and begged him, 'Be patient with me, and I will pay it back.'
> –Matthew 18:28-29 (NIV)

The Self

The self is home to our reputation, interests, passions, plans, likes, dislikes, pleasures, and more…anything that defines us. Psychologists say we have three selves — the public self, the private self, and the ideal self.

10. The public self is the self we take to church, to work, and to other **public** places. This is the self the **world** sees.

11. The private self is the person or self we are when **no** one is **watching**. This is who we are when we are not at church or in a business meeting. It is who we are when we are disappointed, hurt, or betrayed, when we lose our jobs and have unpaid bills, when we are tired and hungry. Often, this is the **real** self.

12. The ideal self is the person or self we **wish** to or should be. Of the three, the **ideal** self is displayed **least**.

13. When Apostle Paul says in 1 Corinthians 15:31, "I die daily", which self is he referring to? **The private self**.

14. What does the following mean in practical terms?

    a. Crucify the flesh (Galatians 5:24). **To reflect Christ, not ourselves, through our behaviors.**

b. Deny self (Luke 9:23). **To not give in or yield to our fleshy desires. For example, when insulted, our flesh will want us to snap back at the person. To answer an insult with a kind word is to deny the self.**

> Then he said to them all: "Whoever wants to be my disciple must deny themselves and take up their cross daily and follow me.
> —Luke 9:23 (NIV)
>
> Submit yourselves therefore to God. Resist the devil, and he will flee from you.
> —James 4:7 (KJV)

c. Die daily (1 Corinthians 15:31). **Examine the self every day and do the necessary with the grace of God to silence it, to make sure its demands are not louder than the demands of the Holy Spirit.**

d. Submit to God. (James 4:7). **Not you will or your way, but God's.**

15. How does the act of forgiveness reflect self-denial? **When we forgive, at a minimum we are denying the self of the right we think we have to retribution and the right we think we have to protect ourselves.**

16. How does submitting to God help us forgive our offenders? **It is God's will / desire that we forgive our offenders, so if we put our desires aside and seek to give God what He wants, we will be submitting to Him. By submitting to Him, we get the strength we need to resist the devil who would be telling us not to forgive our offenders.**

17. Compare physical death with death to self. How do they differ?

a. Physical death — Loss of **natural** life; **separation** of the **spirit** from the mortal body; cessation of natural, mortal existence, but you still die with all your passions, lusts, and desires intact.

b. Death to self — Yielding/**surrendering** of your will/**desires**. You lose your passions, lusts, and desires to God. The nature of Christ superimposes your **nature**, and you now act like **Christ**. When you are dead to self, it is no longer about you but all about the God you serve. When you are dead to self, you are fully **submitted** and completely sold out to God. Therefore, even amid pain and offense, you seek to please your God.

18. Death to self can be very difficult and painful. What would make this process difficult or painful? (Romans 7:15-21). **Death to self will be difficult if we are not submitted to God. If not submitted to God, self will be alive and may manifest itself through pride, seeking self-interest, self-defense, and other ungodly behaviors. Self is ingrained in us. It is a function of how we are wired to operate. It is a combination of our personality and character, so self will resist dying to Christ. Self wants to rule.**

> ➤ *Discuss the quote below and suggest some things that could cause a person to be offended by words spoken against him or her.*

"A dead man or woman does not react to an offense. If we can be offended by the words of others, it only proves that our death to self has not been finished."

—Alice Smith, *Beyond the Veil*

Kill Self Along with Its Passions and Cravings

We must crucify our flesh. This means we must kill the flesh along with its passions and desires. Passions equate to cravings, lusts, urges, thirst, and hunger. We must go deep down in our spirits to the origin of what has gotten us to where we are and uproot these things and kill them, and we must do this every day. This does not sound very gentle or courteous, but if we are to be ruthless and cruel to anything, it should be to self. This means that we cannot live as devoted and holy vessels while oblivious to how we are wired.

With a reasonable understanding of the nature of self and how it operates, we should better understand why we find it so difficult to obey God's commands, even when we say we love Him, have the desire to obey Him, and are very aware of the consequences if we do not obey Him.

Speaking specifically to the focus of this discussion, we will find it completely impossible to obey His command to forgive if we do not deny self. Therefore, there are so many people in the church who struggle with unforgiveness. They have not denied self the right to hold people accountable for what those persons have done to them. So self is the sole reason many cannot say "Yes" to the command to forgive.

We must crucify the flesh. This means we must kill the flesh along with its passions and desires.

Take note of yourself or anyone who is hurt. When they talk, they use a lot of *I* and *me*. They talk primarily about what was done to them and how they feel. Though they are unconscious of this fact, self is their sole focus. When we focus on self, we empower it, and in empowering self, we become less likely or able to do what pleases God. When self is the strong man, we are least likely to obey God. We cannot forgive when self prevails.

Passion means cravings, lusts, urges, thirsts, and hungers. These are all rooted in the very core of our beings.

A *craving* is a deep-seated need to have or do something; it's something you greatly desire to have or do. When we have a craving, we long for the thing we crave. We yearn for it, and as resourceful as we are, we often find a way to satisfy our cravings, even at our expense or the expense of others.

Urges are something we feel we must have. When an urge goes unmet, we think about it all the time. We try to figure out how to get what we have a longing for. If we do not get it, we may substitute something for it, but we will soon find out that it doesn't satisfy the urge, so we're back to where we started, still trying to figure out how to meet that urge.

Lust is another strong term. Lust is generally defined as a very strong sexual desire for someone. But an expanded definition is "an intense desire for anything." It could be power, recognition, knowledge, food—anything.

Cravings, urges, and lusts are all extraordinarily strong terms, but this is what

passion means. We are told in Galatians 5:24 to kill self along with all its passions and desires. They run so deep that it is clear they are a part of us. That is why it is so very difficult to deny self. When self craves or lusts for something, we cannot deny it in our own strengths. These are the passions and desires to which the scripture points. We are required to crucify them, and if we don't, they will control us and hinder us from being obedient to God. They will hinder us from being forgiving to those who offend us.

> ➤ *Discuss the following.*

19. How can a person's *passions* hinder them from forgiving their offender?

20. How can a person's *carvings* hinder them from forgiving their offender?

21. How can a person's *urges* hinder them from forgiving their offender?

22. How can a person's *lusts* hinder them from forgiving their offender?

Alice Smith states that, "*Humility means bringing all you are under His Lordship. It means becoming God-dependent.*"

> ➤ *Discuss the following.*

23. What it means to be God-dependent.

24. What being God-dependent looks like when a person is wronged by another.

25. The extent to which we interpret **offense** as a **personal** assault on our image and our reputation is evidence that we place much esteem and value on the **self**.

End the session with prayer. Suggested prayer points:

1. Passionate love for Christ that will fuel you to put Him first in everything concerning you.

2. A will that is entirely submitted to God. Death to self and alive to Christ.

3. To truly surrender to God — all your passions, urges, lusts, and cravings.

4. To truly making Christ the lord and king of your life.

Reflection and Personal Application

Think carefully. Do you have any passions or desires that make it difficult for you to crucify self? In what areas of your life do you find it difficult to submit to God? Where are you most defensive?

Can you think of anyone you need to forgive? Write down the name(s). Can you see how any of the issues you identified in the previous paragraph could make it difficult for you to forgive?

Now find and write down at least one corresponding scripture that can minister to you about each of the issues you identified. Pray to your heavenly Father for healing from these conditions and for the strength to overpower their negative effects.

Unit 2: The Snare of Unforgiveness

Session 9: It's A Trap

> Offense is a trap, a snare, a stumbling block set by the adversary of our souls to dishonor, shame, and disgrace us.

Session Goals

By the end of this session, participants will
- fully understand the destruction of unforgiveness,
- know the ultimate plan behind offense, and
- know God's perspective on offense.

What Is Unforgiveness?

Unforgiveness is unfulfilled revenge. It is a state of anger, passively or openly expressed,

> *Unforgiveness is unfulfilled revenge.*

toward the person or persons who cause us hurt. Rarely is the anger that is associated with unforgiveness expressed openly among Christians. We are too churchy for openly expressed anger, but that does not mean there is no anger in the Church. It is very present. Anger that is rooted in unforgiveness is present at all levels in the Church, from the pulpit to the pews. Like the members of our local churches, there are pastoral and ministerial staff with unforgiveness in their hearts.

Because unforgiveness can go unnoticed to the naked eye, it has become one of the most prevalent spiritual diseases in the Church. However, in the Church or otherwise, unforgiveness is a deadly spiritual and emotional poison. But unfortunately, many in the body of Christ take this deadly of poisons.

Joyce Meyer puts it this way, "Staying angry at someone who has hurt you is like taking poison hoping that your enemy will die."[1] And I put it this way; "Unforgiveness is a prison built by the offended and the person behind bars is the offended, not the offender." Fundamentally, when we do not forgive, we are not doing the offender any harm. All the harm is done to us.

Unforgiveness is rooted in **anger**.

1. The anger in which unforgiveness is rooted resides in the **offended**.

2. The **offended** is subject to the damage that is caused by the anger.

3. There are two types of anger — **aggressive** and **passive aggressive**.

4. Another word for passive anger is **passive aggression**.

5. Passive aggression is **an indirect** expression of one's **negative** feelings, instead of **openly** addressing them.

6. Identify some expressions of passive anger. **sarcasm, ill will, resentment, hostile jokes, negative criticisms, sullenness, undue silence, procrastination, contradictions, and negative attitudes**.

The price we pay for harboring passive and openly expressed anger is the same. Therefore, hiding animosity in our hearts toward the persons who hurt us instead of openly attacking them or addressing the issue does not spare us the consequences of unforgiveness.

As depicted in figure 3 on page 4, if forgiveness does not occur after the infraction and before hurt sets in or after hurt but before offense sets in, we are on our way to bitterness. The offense referred to here is synonymous with unforgiveness, and it comes about when we harbor the hurt we experienced because of the infraction.

Why Does Hurt Linger?

Several things could cause hurt to linger.

Some people rehearse the incident in their minds — continually thinking of what was said, what happened to them, or what they could have said or done differently.

> ➤ *Discuss the following vignettes.*

Denise's choir director asked her to lead one of the songs they intend on singing at the next service. Denise did her best to practice the song throughout the week. When she got to rehearsal and Sean, the choir director, asked her to sing the part, she gave it her best. She thought she did an excellent job, but Sean openly insulted her and told her she was croaking. He said the version of the song she was singing is different from what he had in mind, and he did not like it. Denise was embarrassed and very hurt. She could barely sing during the rest of the rehearsal.

She left the rehearsal with a heavy heart. She could not stop thinking about how humiliating that was. She started thinking about all the flaws in Sean's leadership, for example, he does not know how to encourage and appreciate people, and he disrespects people. Furthermore, he did not give her the version of the song that he wanted her to practice. She thought a lot about what she should have said to him when he degraded her and regretted not lashing back at him. In her mind, if he could do that in front of the entire choir, she should answer back in like manner in front of the choir. The entire week, it seemed as if all she could think about was what happened and what she should have done to defend herself.

7. List some emotions that could accompany Denise's recollection/pondering of what happened at the choir rehearsal. **pain, regret, shame, resentment, anger, and intimidation**.

8. Are any of these emotions positive? **No**.

> *Hurt after an infraction against us is normal, but sustained hurt is not normal. This leads to offense, which I call unforgiveness.*

Some people who have been hurt by another person take every chance they get to retell their story, and usually the story is not a testament of the great work of God in their hearts or in the situation. It is typically a reiteration of what happened to them. By retelling the story so many times, they know the details. That is exactly what Satan wants. He wants the incident to mark our memories so that we never get over it.

Telling and retelling the story only deepens the roots of the pain and hurt in our spirits. If we retell the incident as a testament of how God brought us out and changed our lives, it will not deepen the hurt. Instead, it will bring deliverance to the hearers. Retelling the story causes the hurt to linger. Hurt also lingers because the offended is self-centered.

Denise has told herself that she will never forget what Sean did to her. Every time she sees him, especially at rehearsal, she remembers what happened. In fact, since then she has not accepted any offers to sing the lead on a song. Every opportunity Denise gets; she refers to her experience with Sean. This sometimes happens in the fellowship hall and even in Bible studies. If the topic is on anything that gives an opening for her to share this experience, she takes full advantage of the opportunity. She may or may not use his name, but undoubtedly, she references the story or relates it in full detail. Whenever she is in a conversation with her peers from church and any talk regarding the things about the church with which they are happy and unhappy comes up, Denise is sure to go into full detail about what happened between her and Sean. Years later, Denise still would retell her story at every opportunity, and not one of those storytelling occasions was a testimony of victory or thanksgiving to God.

Denise is totally humiliated. She is adamant that Sean disrespected her, does not appreciate all the sacrifices she has made to serve in the choir, and fails to acknowledge that she sings very well. She also attests that Sean is the one who is wrong because he did not give her the music for the song he wanted her to practice. Denise demands an apology. She will not sing another lead if Sean does not apologize. In fact, Denise is contemplating resigning from the choir.

9. Given how Denise is handling the situation, what are some emotions that may accompany her recollection/pondering of what happened at the choir rehearsal? **pain, regret, resentment, and anger**.

10. Are any of these emotions positive? **No**. Could there be any positive emotions? **No, not likely**.

11. Do you think Denise has forgiven Sean? Why? Why not? **No**.

12. Does retelling the story help the hearers? How does retelling the story affect Denise?

13. What are some of the possible implications when Denise rehashes the story with other members of the church?

14. What are some of the possible implications if Denise rehashes the story with unbelievers?

15. With what kind of heart condition do you think Denise retells her story? **anger, hurt, need for revenge**.

16. Which type of anger is expressed when Denise retells the story? Discuss why it's one type of aggression/anger—passive aggressive or aggressive—and not the other. **passive aggressive**.

17. What do you think Denise's real motive (whether she is aware of it or not) is for retelling her story?

God's Perspective on Offense

18. The Greek word for **offense** is *skándalon*, a noun. The future tense verb form is *skandalizo*. The English words **scandal** and **scandalize** come directly from these Greek words.

19. Based on this exposition, when we are offended, we expose ourselves to a **scandal**, something of dishonor, shame, and disgrace.

20. The New American Standard (NAS) Exhaustive Concordance defines *skándalon* as a **snare**, a **stumbling block**, an **offense**.

21. Thayer's Greek Lexicon, Strong's New Testament (#4625) defines *skándalon* as a rock that is a cause of **stumbling**.

22. According to Biblehub.com (http://biblehub.com/greek/4625.htm), *skándalon* has several meanings:

   a. The trigger of a **trap**. The mechanism that closes a trap down on the unsuspecting victim, an offense.
   b. The means of **stumbling**; the means of **entrapment**.
   c. The bait-stick of a trap, a **snare**, a stumbling-block (Abbott-Smith).

23. What two common threads run through these definitions? (1) skándalon (or offense) is a **trap**; and (2) an obstruction that causes one to **stumble**.

> A brother wronged is more unyielding than a fortified city; disputes are like the barred gates of a citadel.
> —Proverbs 18:19 (NIV)
>
> A brother offended is harder to be won than a strong city: and their contentions are like the bars of a castle.
> —Proverbs 18:19 (KJV)

It is clear here that offense is a trap that Satan sets to catch the saints. He catches us because we are unaware that the trap is set. If we know a trap is set, we will go around it or not go in that direction. But because we are unaware of Satan's devices, he catches us in the trap of offense, and the longer we stay in the trap or the longer we stay offended, the closer we come to dying. Simply put, the trap of offense leads to spiritual death.

➤ *Discuss in practical terms (give examples) how offense could be a scandal, a trap, a stumbling block, or an obstruction.*

24. Using Proverbs 18:19, describe Denise in the scenario below.
   Consider key words and phrases such as *unyielding, fortified city, barred gates, harder to be won,* and *contentions.*

Denise is very hurt by what Sean (the choir director) did to her. She has stopped attending choir rehearsal and has not said anything to Sean about her absence. Whenever she is at church and the choir ministers, or if Sean is doing anything, she leaves the sanctuary. In fact, Denise now attends church irregularly, she often arrives late, and she keeps to herself and does not fellowship with her peers as she normally did. A few caring brethren in the church have tried to give her godly counsel, but the conversation always tuns into her communicating what Sean did to her and how much she is hurt and embarrassed and feels unappreciated. It has gotten to the point that it's better to not say anything to her because every occasion becomes an opportunity for her to vent and push people farther away from her.

25. In the eyes of the offended, they are always **right**.

26. In the eyes of the offended, the offender is always **wrong**.

27. While in the trap of offense, we solely focus on the **offense**.

28. It is difficult to get through to an offended person because their new mission is to make sure they never get **hurt** again.

29. Hurt people make sure they never get hurt again by building **contentious walls** around them and close out everyone.

30. These **walls** separate the offended from others and create a **lonely** place, a place of slow **death**.

31. Did Sean handle the situation correctly? **No**

32. Does Denise have a right to feel hurt, embarrassed, and unappreciated? **Yes**

33. Is she handling the situation, right? If yes, why? If not, how could she better handle the situation? **She is not handling the situation right. She should start by talking to Sean first; not to argue but to correct the wrong. If Sean admits to his wrong, they could make peace then. If not, she should try to address the issue with him and a trusted mature brother or sister in the Lord.**

34. According to Scripture, how should Denise handle this situation? Consider Matthew 7:1-5, Ephesians 4:1-3, and Colossians 3:12-13.

a. Matthew 7:1-5— **Examine herself instead of focusing on Sean's wrongdoing.**

b. Ephesians 4:1-3— **Make sure she is doing the right thing and not rendering evil for evil. Show forbearance for Sean's shortcoming and do her best to maintain peace between her and Sean.**

c. Colossians 3:12-13— **Be humble about the whole issue and be kind to Sean, even though he was not kind to her. Forgive him.**

When we isolate ourselves from others, physically or emotionally, we build our own place of slow death. Isn't that what Satan wants? Yes! He wants us offended so that spiritual death can be our fate. And he is crafty enough to make this death slow and unnoticeable to you and to others. That is why so many offended people are in our pews and pulpits. They are offended and dying slowly, yet they continue to function in their capacities or continue to attend church as if nothing is wrong.

This takes us back to a central Bible verse in this study: 2 Corinthians 2:11 — *"in order that Satan might not outwit us. For we are not unaware of his schemes."* We must be aware of the schemes of Satan. Do not let him trap you with offense. It is slow but sure death.

[1] Do not judge, or you too will be judged. [2] For in the same way you judge others, you will be judged, and with the measure you use, it will be measured to you. [3] "Why do you look at the speck of sawdust in your brother's eye and pay no attention to the plank in your own eye? [4] How can you say to your brother, 'Let me take the speck out of your eye,' when all the time there is a plank in your own eye? [5] You hypocrite, first take the plank out of your own eye, and then you will see clearly to remove the

End the session with prayer. Suggested prayer points:

1. Increased awareness of the plan of the enemy toward you and, conversely, the plan of God toward you.

2. Increased awareness of the subtle ways in which the enemy works.

3. Strength and grace to not allow yourself to be offended, despite the infraction against you.

4. The will to forgive anyone you need to forgive.

Reflection and Personal Application

Think carefully. Have you been hurt by anyone? You are fully aware that you need to forgive the person, but you cannot seem to find the strength to do so. You are offended. You find it difficult to forgive the person because the person did you wrong and nothing has been done about it. You are hurt, but at the same time, you are trapped by Satan in the claws of offense.

Ask yourself the following: (1) Specifically what did the person do that has hurt me so badly? (2) Why does this thing hurt so badly? (3) Is there anything about me that needs to change so that, should the same thing happen to me in the future, it won't hurt as badly as it does now or maybe not at all?

Pray to your heavenly Father about whatever you identified that needs to change. Ask God to heal you in that place or those places. These are broken, wounded places in your spirit that only God, your healer, can restore. Be open and honest about your feelings with your Father. He wants to hear the desires of your heart coming from your own lips. When you pray, accept His healing, even before you see the manifestation. Declare over yourself that your spirit and emotions are made whole and begin to think about yourself that way. This will be followed by healthy changes in your behavior.

Unforgiveness is a prison built by the offended, and the person behind bars is the offended, not the offender.

Session Goal

By the end of this session, participants will learn of the high price we pay when we do not forgive.

The Cost Is High

Without a doubt, unforgiveness comes at an extremely high spiritual cost. If not dealt with, unforgiveness can cost us everything — our destiny and our ultimate destination after this life. If we do not forgive, we are heading to eternal doom with Satan.

Among the costs of unforgiveness are the following:
> ▶ Prevents God from forgiving our sins.
> ▶ Opens us up to tormentors (the devil).
> ▶ Blocks God from answering our prayers.
> ▶ Defiles us.

▶ **Prevents God from Forgiving Our Sins**

1. Discuss the following scriptures.
a. Romans 3:23— **Everyone has sinned. None of us are fully pleasing to God.**
b. Matthew 6:15— **We must forgive others to be forgiven of our sins.**

c. 1 John 1:9— **God is faithful, and we can depend on Him to forgive us of our sins. He will make our lives clean from all sin**.

2. Is there such a thing as a sinless person? **No**.

3. Who needs forgiveness from God? **Everyone**.

4. If we sin, are we likely to ask God to forgive us? **Yes**

5. Is there ever a time when God does not forgive us, if yes, under what circumstance does He not forgive us?

6. What happens if we do not forgive those who offend us? **We will not receive forgiveness from God when we ask of Him.**

7. Is forgive or not forgive ever conditional? Is it ever acceptable not to forgive our offender? Why? Why not?

> *Everyone sins; therefore, we all need forgiveness from God. But if we do not forgive others, He will not forgive us. That is an extremely high price to pay for unforgiveness.*

> [24] As he began the settlement, a man who owed him ten thousand bags of gold[h] was brought to him. [25] Since he was not able to pay, the master ordered that he and his wife and his children and all that he had be sold to repay the debt. [26] "At this the servant fell on his knees before him. 'Be patient with me,' he begged, 'and I will pay back everything.'
> —Matthew 18:24-26 (NIV)

►Opens Us Up to Tormentors (the Devil)

Read Matthew 18:23-35. Jesus told a remarkably interesting parable here about an unforgiving/unmerciful servant. Here we have a king who wanted to reconcile his accounts with his servants. As he was doing so, he realized he had a servant who owed him a huge debt. Another servant owed this servant pittance compared to what he owed his lord.

8. How much did the servant owe the king? (Matthew 18:24): **10,000 talents**.

9. Was the servant able to pay the debt? **No**

10. What was the servant's response when the lord asked for what was owed to him? (Matthew 18:26). **He was not able to pay the debt. The servant fell on his knees before the king and begged, "Be patient with me and I will pay back everything."**

11. One talent is equal to **6,000 denarii**, which would take an ordinary laborer then **6,000 days** (nearly seventeen years) to earn. According to the American Standard Version (ASV) of the Bible, a talent was worth about one thousand dollars; therefore, this servant owed the lord **10 million dollars**, or **60 million denarii**.

When the servant stood before his lord, he asked for patience and stated that he would repay the debt. *"Have patience with me, and I will pay all that I owe"* (Matthew 18:26). This was unrealistic because according to Matthew 20:2, the daily wage of a working man in Palestine then was "a shilling," about seventeen cents. Based on this, it would take the servant well over one thousand (1,611.6) years to pay off this ten-million-dollar debt with a wage of seventeen cents per day if every cent he earned was used to help pay off the debt.

12. What was the king's response? (Matthew 18:25b, 27) **He had mercy on the servant and canceled the debt instead of having him (and his wife and children and all that he had) sold to repay the debt**.

13. The servant later found a fellow servant who owed him. How much was the servant owed by this fellow servant? (Matthew 18:26) **100 denarii or silver coins**.

14. What did the servant do to the fellow servant when he found him? (Matthew 18:28) **He grabbed the fellow servant and began to choke him, demanding his money**.

15. What was the fellow servant's response? **When the unmerciful servant asked the fellow servant to pay what was owed to him, the fellow servant fell to his knees and begged him to be patient and he would repay him.**

16. Was the response of the fellow servant to the unmerciful servant any different from the unmerciful servant's response to the lord? **The response of the unmerciful servant to the lord was no different from the response of the fellow servant to the unmerciful servant**.

17. What was the servant's response to the fellow servant's plea? (Matthew 18:30) **He refused and had the fellow servant thrown into prison until he could pay the debt.**

18. What did the king do when he heard of this? **The lord called in the unmerciful servant and said to him, "You wicked servant! I forgave you all that debt because you begged me. Shouldn't you also have had mercy on your fellow servant, even as I had mercy on you?" (Matthew 18:32 NIV). The lord became angry and handed the unmerciful servant over to the tormentors until he could pay all that was due to the lord**.

19. The king represents **God**.

20. The unmerciful servant represents **Us**.

> 27 The servant's master took pity on him, canceled the debt and let him go. 28 "But when that servant went out, he found one of his fellow servants who owed him a hundred silver coins. He grabbed him and began to choke him. 'Pay back what you owe me!' he demanded. 30 "But he refused. Instead, he went off and had the man thrown into prison until he could pay the debt. 32 "Then the master called the servant in. 'You wicked servant,' he said, 'I canceled all that debt of yours because you begged me to.'
> —Matthew 18:27-28, 30, 32 (NIV)

21. The debt owed to the lord represents our **sins**.

22. Has God forgiven us of our sins? **Yes**

23. Can we pay God for the forgiveness of our sins? **No**

> *If God can forgive us of such a debt, why can't we forgive the pittance owed to us?*

The debt owed to the unmerciful servant compared to a ten-million-dollar debt was nothing. His servant owed him one hundred shillings, about seventeen dollars. In this parable, the king represents God and the indebted servant pictures each of us in the state of unforgiveness. The offenses that our brothers and sisters cause us are likened to the seventeen-dollar debt owed to the unmerciful servant, and our transgressions against God's Word is likened to the ten-million-dollar debt to the lord. We can never pay that debt. God has forgiven us, and Jesus continues to make intercession for us (Hebrews 7:25). He died for us while we were sinners, and before we knew we needed a savior (Romans 5:8). So, if God can forgive us of such a debt, why can't we forgive the pittance owed to us?

Pay close attention to the lord's reaction and what he did to the unmerciful servant when he learned of what the servant did to his fellow servant. He became angry and gave him over to the tormentors. God will do the same thing to us if we do not forgive our brothers and sisters of their misdeeds. When we do not forgive, God is not pleased with us, and He will remove the hedge so that the tormentors can have their way with us.

▶ Blocks God from Answering Our Prayers

Read Mark 11:25.

24. When we come to pray, if we find that we have anything in our heart against anyone, what should we do? **Forgive them**.

25. In doing so, what will our Father in heaven do? **He will forgive us of our sins.**

26. Read Psalm 66:18. Discuss the condition (if/then situation) described in this verse. ***If* we don't forgive others, *then* God won't hear our prayers. He won't hear our prayers for forgiveness**.

> *Discuss this question: Is the risk worth taking?*

> And when you stand praying, if you hold anything against anyone, forgive them, so that your Father in heaven may forgive you your sins.
> —Mark 11:25 (NIV)
>
> If I regard iniquity in my heart, the Lord will not hear me:
> —Psalm 66:18 (KJV)

▶Defiles Us

Unforgiveness and any form of bitterness is sin, and sin defiles us. Read Hebrews 12:15.

> Looking diligently lest any man fail of the grace of God; lest any root of bitterness springing up trouble you, and thereby many be defiled;
> —Hebrews 12:15 (KJV)

27. The root of bitterness is likened to **unforgiveness**.

28. This root of bitterness/unforgiveness can (1) cause us **trouble** and (2) **defile many**.

➢ *Discuss how unforgiveness in a person can defile others/many. Consider Luke 6:45 in your discussion.*

Unforgiving people are angry and hurt. That is the condition of their hearts. Therefore, their words are often coined in anger and pain. Speaking words of anger about anyone within the hearing of others can influence how the hearers perceive the people that are spoken of. Everyone that hears these unkind words spoken by the unforgiving person can become defiled and can, in turn, repeat those words to others; therefore, perpetuate these negative notions and, as a result, defile many.

> A good man brings good things out of the good stored up in his heart, and an evil man brings evil things out of the evil stored up in his heart. For the mouth speaks what the heart is full of.
> —Luke 6:45 (NIV)

End the session with prayer. Suggested prayer points:

1. For your heart to be filled with the love of God so that offense and unforgiveness will never be an issue for you

2. A heart of compassion and mercy toward others, even those who hurt you.

3. A heart like that of the lord who had mercy on the servant, like your heavenly Father has toward you.

4. A life or heart condition that positions you to be used by God and opens the heavens and throne of grace to your prayers.

Reflection and Personal Application

Matthew 18 is the central scripture in this lesson. Read it slowly and carefully. Think about how you relate to others and how your heavenly Father relates to you. Does your heavenly Father forgive you of debts you cannot repay? Does He have a limit on forgiving you? Does He at any time not forgive you because, in His opinion, He has forgiven you sufficiently, perhaps in general or for a specific issue?

Now think about how you relate to others. Is there a limit on the things for which you are willing to forgive others? Are you more willing to forgive them of some things versus others? Is there a limit to how many times you will forgive a person, in general or for a specific issue?

Where the answers differ about God and about you are highlights of the condition of your heart. These are issues I am encouraging you to take to the One who loves you the most, the One who loves you more than any other person can love you, even yourself. Talk to Him about these issues and ask Him to build you up spiritually so that you can operate like Him and so that you can treat others as He treats you. Do not expect immediate results. This will be a process that you must conscientiously work toward. With the help of the Holy Spirit, you can do it.

Unforgiveness hardens our hearts, makes us self-centered and merciless, and makes us completely ungrateful to God for His mercies toward us.

Session Goal

By the end of this session, participants will learn of the high price we pay when we do not forgive.

The Cost Is High

We will continue our study of the consequences of unforgiveness in this session. As a review, the four consequences that were highlighted in the previous session are (1) prevents God from forgiving our sins, (2) opens us up to tormentors, (the devil), (3) blocks God from answering our prayers, and (4) defiles us.

The remaining consequences we will discuss are as follows:

- ▶ Gives Satan an advantage.
- ▶ Opens us up to curses.
- ▶ Prevents us from entering the kingdom of God.
- ▶ Makes us vulnerable to physical illness and disease.
- ▶ Prevents us from spiritual fruitfulness.

▶ Gives Satan an Advantage

Read 2 Corinthians 2:10-11

When we do not forgive others, we give Satan an advantage over us, a foothold in our lives. This foothold, if not dealt with, can become a stronghold over time. According to the apostle Paul, one way to make sure Satan does not have an advantage over us is to forgive. *Anyone you forgive, I also forgive. And what I have forgiven—if there was anything to forgive—I have forgiven in the sight of Christ for your sake, in order that Satan might not outwit us. For we are not unaware of his schemes* (2 Corinthians 2:10-11). The key phrase here is *in order that*. This indicates that we forgive *so that* Satan does not have an advantage over us. When we do not forgive, we give Satan an advantage over us. Unforgiveness puts us in Satan's trap, and there he can do with us whatever he sees fit.

> ➤ *Discuss what "in order that" and "so that" mean. Give practical examples to explain both phrases.*

> [10] Anyone you forgive, I also forgive. And what I have forgiven—if there was anything to forgive—I have forgiven in the sight of Christ for your sake, [11] in order that Satan might not outwit us. For we are not unaware of his schemes.
> —2 Corinthians 2:10-11 (NIV)

►Opens Us Up to Curses

Read Deuteronomy 27:26 and Matthew 18:34.

1. Does our loving heavenly Father ever curse anyone? If yes, under what circumstances? **Anyone who does not uphold the words of the laws of God by carrying them out is cursed** (Deuteronomy 27:26).

We also see in Matthew 18:34 that the lord gave the unmerciful servant over to the tormentors. When the lord found out that the servant did not forgive his fellow servant, he became angry and gave him over to the tormentors. That's a curse.

Tormenting spirits are always lurking around, looking for opportunities. When we walk in obedience to God, His hedge of protection is airtight, making it impossible for tormenting spirits to attack us. Unforgiveness, on the other hand, breaks the hedge. Tormenting spirits have direct access to us when we do not forgive. That was the unmerciful servant's fate because he did not forgive his fellow servant. There is no blessing in unforgiveness. Unforgiveness is disobedience to God's words, and God does not bless disobedience.

2. Is what the lord did for the unforgiving servant in Matthew 18:34 applicable to the unforgiving individual now, later, or both? **Now and later**.

3. If now, what could be some manifestations of being given over to tormentors? **A life that's devoid of peace—complaining, negative, vindictive, argumentative, contentious**.

►Prevents Us from Entering the Kingdom of God

If God does not hear our prayers when we pray with iniquity (unforgiveness) in our hearts (Psalm 66:18), and if He does not forgive us if we do not forgive others (Matthew 6:15), it means that if we are walking in unforgiveness we cannot expect to enter the kingdom of God.

4. What do the following scriptures say about this?

5. Galatians 6:7— Whatever a man **sows**, that he will also **reap**. Therefore, if we sow unforgiveness, we reap **unforgiveness**.

6. Matthew 7:21— Only those who do the **will** of God, who is in heaven, will enter the kingdom of **heaven**. Unforgiveness is not in the will of our Father. Therefore, **unforgiveness** disqualifies us from entering the kingdom of God.

▶ Makes Us Vulnerable to Physical Illness and Disease

Unforgiveness is a sin, and sin can cause sickness. Read Psalm 41:3-4.

> The Lord sustains them on their sickbed and restores them from their bed of illness. I said, "Have mercy on me, Lord; heal me, for I have sinned against you."
>
> —Psalm 41:3–4

Here we see David asking God to have mercy on him, to heal him from physical illness, from his bed of illness, for he had sinned against God. If unforgiveness is a sin, this verse tells us that the sin of unforgiveness can confine us to a bed of illness.

An unforgiving heart gives access to the enemy of our souls. When the enemy attacks, no sphere of influence is off limits unless guarded by the Holy Spirit Himself. Remember, the unforgiving person has gone outside of the hedge of protection, giving Satan ready access.

According to a study by Worthington and colleagues, unforgiveness is "a combination of delayed negative emotions (i.e., resentment, bitterness, hostility, hatred, anger, and fear) toward a transgressor"[2] Essentially, unforgiveness is a stress response with potential health consequences.

Unforgiving people are not at peace with themselves or with others. Lack of peace equates to anxiety and unrest, which spills over to other domains of their lives, including their physical health. Anxiety often has a myriad of physical implications, such as insomnia, hypertension, chemical imbalance, muscle tension, migraine, acid reflux, and ulcer, to name a few.

Several years ago, a study done by researchers associated with the National Comorbidity Study obtained data from a sample of slightly more than 6,500 US residents, who responded to the statement, "Would you say this is true or false? I've held grudges against people for years."

Those who said they tended to hold grudges reported higher rates of heart disease and cardiac arrest, elevated blood pressure, stomach ulcers, arthritis, back problems, headaches, and chronic pain than those who did not have this tendency.[3]

Unforgiveness puts our physical health at risk. It wounds our souls, making us more vulnerable to being sick. A lot of us have physical ailments because of unforgiveness.

7. What do these scriptures say about emotional brokenness and physical health?

a. Proverbs 12:25— Anxiety **weighs down the heart**, but a kind word cheers it up.

b. Proverbs 15:13— A happy heart **makes the face cheerful**, but heartache **crushes the spirit**.

▶ Prevents Us from Being Spiritually Fruitful

Unforgiveness or offense in the Church causes division. This is not what Jesus prayed for in John 17. He prayed *"that we would be one, so that the world would know that God sent Him into the world to save the lost"* (John 17:21). An inherent result of offense is division, and this misrepresents Christ to the world.

> *Our self-centeredness, expressed through offense, stands in the way of the salvation of the lost, rendering us unfruitful.*

It is through the Church — not the buildings but the people that make up the body — that the world will come to know Jesus. God is love. *"He loves the entire human race—all creeds, races, and class—that is why He sent His only Son to die in our place"* (John 3:16, emphasis added). However, when we are divided, we do an extremely poor job at representing Him to the world.

When we are divided, we do not portray His love. When we are offended, we literally stand between the Savior of the world and the lost. The price is lost souls. Our self-centeredness, expressed through offense, stands in the way of the salvation of the lost, rendering us unfruitful.

Spiritual fruitfulness is used in scripture as an indicator of spiritual maturity and well-being. Spiritual fruitfulness is an expectation that is placed upon God's people. Our measure of fruitfulness is in Galatians 5:22-23: love, joy, peace, forbearance, kindness, goodness, faithfulness, gentleness, and self-control.

8. Of the nine aspects of the fruit of the Spirit, which one(s) do you think an unforgiving person lacks most? Why? **The best way to reflect Christ is to love like He loves. So, of the nine aspects of the fruit of the Spirit, the one that the unforgiving person lacks most may be love. Another is peace because the unforgiving lives with the memory and the pain of the wrong that was done to them.**

> But the fruit of the Spirit is love, joy, peace, longsuffering, gentleness, goodness, faith, [23] Meekness, temperance: against such there is no law.
> —Galatians 5:22-23 (KJV)

Read 1 Corinthians 13:5; John 15:12; John 14:15, 24; and Psalm 119:165.

9.   What evidence, if any, is in 1 Corinthians 13:5 and John 15:12 that love is a fruit of forgiveness?

a.   1 Corinthians 13:5— **Love does not keep a record of wrongs. It is evident that unforgiving individuals do not have love because they keep record of the misdeeds done to them by recalling and retelling them.**

b.   John 15:12— **Jesus commands us to love one another, as He has loved us. True love does not hold bitterness or unforgiveness against another. If we are bitter or holding unforgiveness against our brothers and sisters, then we do not love them as Christ loves us.**

c.   John 14:15, 24— **If we do not keep Jesus' commandments, then it proves we do not love Him either. Our love for God is questionable when we cannot forgive. Unforgiveness shows we don't really love Jesus as we say we do. John 14:24 says, "Anyone who does not love me will not obey my teaching," and John 14:15 says, "If ye love me, keep my commandments." Unforgiveness is evidence that we do not love God as we say we do.**

10.   Psalm 119:165— Why would peace be a fruit of being forgiving? **Peace and unforgiveness cannot coexist. They are mutually exclusive. The unforgiving cannot be at peace because the real reason for unforgiveness is a desire for revenge or restitution. As long as that desire is not met, the unforgiving will not be at peace but will be angry.**

It does not dishonor others, it is not self-seeking, it is not easily angered, it keeps no record of wrongs.
—1 Corinthians 13:5 (NIV)

This is my commandment, That ye love one another, as I have loved you.
John 15:12 (KJV)

15 If you love me, keep my commands. 24 Anyone who does not love me will not obey my teaching. These words you hear are not my own; they belong to the Father who sent me.
—John 14:15, 24

Great peace have those who love your law, and nothing can make them stumble.
—Psalm 119:165

> *Unforgiveness breeds in the polluted conditions of bad memories.*

Unforgiveness breeds in the polluted conditions of bad memories. The more we recall and rehearse the misdeed done against us, the deeper the roots of unforgiveness will penetrate our spirits.

Unforgiveness is a form of deception. While being deceived, we lose a lot of time because our focus is on what happened to us instead of seeking God for the fullness of His will to be done in our lives. Inevitable damage and loss to the unforgiving person is the result of unforgiveness. Unforgiveness is toxic— spiritually, physically, and emotionally. Too much is at stake not to forgive.

End the session with prayer. Suggested prayer points:

1. That your heart to be filled with the love of God so that offense and unforgiveness will never be an issue for you.

2. The peace of God.

3. A life that bears the fruit of the Spirit.

4. That your physical health will never be compromised because of unforgiveness.

5. That Satan will never have an advantage over you because of unforgiveness.

6. That you will never pay a price for unforgiveness.

Reflection and Personal Application

Identify one potential spiritual, emotional, and physical price that is associated with unforgiveness. Identify at least one scripture or Bible-based approach that you or anyone can take to address each issue.

Write out a short prayer in which you ask the Lord to search your heart and show you any trace of unforgiveness or bitterness that is hidden in you.

> Bitterness is harbored hurt and resentment that are privately tucked away and locked up in the soul.

Session Goal

By the end of this session, participants will

- have a better understanding of what bitterness is,
- learn how bitterness is often expressed, and
- learn about passive-aggression.

Unforgiveness versus Bitterness

One could liken unforgiveness to an acute spiritual disease that if not treated, will become chronic, and bitterness to an already chronic disease. The consequences of bitterness are long-lasting, and they get worse over time if not addressed. Bitterness only extends the duration of confinement in the same prison called unforgiveness that the offended has built for him or herself.

Bitter people have been bitten by the infraction and their mission is to bite back. So, they go through life spewing out death and negativity. According to Proverbs 18:21a (KJV) "*Death and life are in the power of the tongue*." Bitter people speak death, not life. They snap at others. Bitter people feed their grudges. They are stuck in anger.

Bitterness is hardened anger. This is not just the anger experienced at the unforgiveness stage, this is anger that has been in place over time and is now solidified (See figure 3 on page 4).

1.   Can a person be bitter but forgiving? **No**

2.   Can a person be unforgiving and not bitter? **Yes**

3.   What is the main distinction between unforgiveness and bitterness? **Unforgiveness** precedes **bitterness**. Bitterness is the result of long-standing **unforgiveness**. Usually, unforgiveness is due to an incident, but bitterness is the root of ill feelings, of anger. So, **bitterness** characterizes the person, their whole outlook on persons and situations.

A Closer Look at Bitterness

Bitterness is that feeling of hurt, resentment, anger, hate, and revenge — passive or active — that builds up in the heart of the person who feels they have been bitten by certain experiences of life. Bitterness stains the carriers' quality of life with resentment. It becomes who they are. Bitter people are not just angry at their offender, they are angry at the world, it's who they are.

> *Bitterness is hardened anger, and many people handle their anger thru passive-aggressive behaviors. Passive-aggression is associated with hidden anger.*

4. What is passive anger? **Indirect** expression of **negative** feelings instead of openly addressing them. There is a disconnect between what a passive-aggressive person **says** and what he or she **does**.

For example, a passive-aggressive person might appear to agree — perhaps even enthusiastically — with another person's request. Rather than complying with the request, however, he or she might express anger or resentment by failing to follow through or missing deadlines.

Specific signs of passive-aggressive behavior include:
- Resentment and opposition to the requests of others.
- Procrastination and intentional mistakes in response to others' requests.
- Cynical, critical, sullen, insulting, or hostile attitude.
- Frequent complaints about feeling underappreciated or cheated.

5. Read the vignette below and discuss which of the two ladies — Doris or Veronica — is bitter.

Doris and Veronica are both married to abusive husbands. Their husbands are controlling, and they abuse them verbally and emotionally. The husbands also degrade them and are very careful to remind them quite frequently that no one will ever marry them if they leave because they are not worth it. Both women's self-esteem is at an all-time low; they feel worthless. Also, they feel trapped for several reasons — they feel helpless. And to make matters worse, the church they attend looks down on separation, let alone divorce.

Doris vows that she is going to divorce her husband no matter what and will have nothing to do with men again. She expresses her disillusion with marriage because she expected her husband to value her and treat her like a queen. She seems to have nothing good to say about men. In any setting if conversations about men come up, she calls them any number of derogatory names that come to mind. She even goes as far as discouraging young ladies from marrying if she gets the opportunity.

Veronica has gotten to the point where she cannot trust her husband and does not believe anything he says to her. After episodes of abuse, her husband often apologizes and tries to be overly kind. But Veronica puts up a wall to shield herself from being hurt again. She is very suspicious of him and is cold towards him. And she does not give ear to his meaningless apologies.

a. Which of the two women is bitter? Why? **Doris is bitter because her anger is not only directed towards her husband, but to men in general. This is the evidence of the root of bitterness.**

b. Which one is unforgiving? Why? **Veronica is unforgiving because she has distanced herself from her husband. She does not listen to, let alone accept his apologies. Her behavior reflects that of a person who is deeply hurt.**

c. What is the main difference noted here between bitterness and unforgiveness? **Bitterness (Doris' behavior) is generalized. Her behavior is not just focused on her husband. Her behavior has become who she is. Veronica's behavior on the other hand is focused on her husband. It has not broadened to men in general. She is still holding her husband, and him only, for what he has done or is doing to her.**

Erroneously, many in the Church believe it is a Christlike thing to not confront or dealing with anger or pain from being hurt by another. Instead of talking about what is making them angry, they suppress it and run the risk of underhandedly sabotaging the person or circumstance that is making them unhappy. It is a very unhealthy behavior and one that can seriously damage relationships.

There are several things a person can do to change their unhealthy patterns of passive-aggressive behavior:

6. Recognize when you feel **angry** and be **honest** about your **anger**.

7. Be assertive and **open** about your **feelings**. When appropriate, **tell** people when they have made you angry.

8. Recognize for yourself when you are **behaving** in a way that is inconsistent with how you are **feeling** and try to **stop** the behavior.

9. Recognize that it is ok to have **disagreements**, to say **no**, and to tell others when they make you **angry**.

10. Learn to **compromise**. It's not black and white; it's not always one person's way or the other. Try to find a comfortable **middle** ground from which you can comfortably **express** yourself.

11. What does Hebrews 12:15 say about bitterness?

    a.   **It is not readily seen**.

    b.   **It is buried in the soul**.

    c.   **It causes trouble**.

    d.   **It can defile many**.

> See to it that no one falls short of the grace of God and that no bitter root grows up to cause trouble and defile many.
> —Hebrews 12:15 (NIV)
>
> For I perceive that thou art in the gall of bitterness, and in the bond of iniquity.
> —Acts 8:23 (KJV)

12. The Old English source of the word "bitterness" is bitan, meaning "to **bite**."

    a.   Bitterness makes a person unfriendly and **bite** at (mean to) others.

    b.   Bitter people become bitter because of the **bite** from the infraction done to them.

13. Acts 8:23— The word gall means **poison**. Bitterness is a **venom**, it is **poisonous**.

Get Rid of Bitterness

14. To get rid of bitterness, you must **uproot** it. You cannot control what happens **to** you, but you can control what happens **in** you. You can control what goes **inside** of you and you should because it is what comes out of the body that **defiles** it.

End the session with prayer. Suggested prayer points:

1. To acknowledge when you are hurt and angry.

2. The openness to deal with your feelings in a healthy, not in a passive aggressive manner.

3. If there is any, the removal of bitterness from the root of your heart.

4. The love of God in your heart will cover all transgressions against you and there will be no room for bitterness.

Reflection and Personal Application

Bitterness is unresolved, unforgiven anger and resentment. It is the result of lingering unaddressed anger. Bitterness is seething and constant. Bitter people carry the same burdens as angry people, but to a greater extent. Bitterness does not affect only you; it affects everyone with whom you interact.

Examine yourself! Are you bitter? If there are any traces of bitterness in your heart, write down the names of those your behavior due to being bitter is likely to affect. Now write out a plan describing how you plan to change your behavior.

> Forgiveness is a choice. As children of God, however, we really have no choice. Yet many of us make the self-destructing decision to withhold forgiveness from those who hurt us.

Session Goal

By the end of this session, participants will

- know the definition of forgiveness God's way, and
- address a few poignant questions about forgiveness.

What Is Forgiveness?

For us to obey God's command to forgive, we must have a clear understanding of what it is. We must know what God says about it. So, what is forgiveness?

When we forgive someone, we write off or pardon the act that was done against us. It is as if a debt was owed to us, and we cancel the debt. Therefore, the debtor no longer owes us anything. When we forgive, the offender owes us nothing, not even an apology.

Forgiveness is freely given to the offender by the offended; it is a gift of love. Those who offend us should not have to ask us to forgive them. They should not have to apologize to us for us to forgive them.

1. When someone offends us, it is likened to a **debt** that is owed to us. When we **forgive** that person, it is likened to **canceling** a debt owed to us.

2. After **forgiving**, the offender owes us **nothing**. It is as if the infraction **never** happened.

3. **Forgiveness** is a **gift** from the **offended** to the offender.

4. Forgiveness is a gift of **love**.

5. Forgiveness is **unconditional**. Not even an **apology** from the offender is **necessary** for forgiveness.

➤ *Discuss the following questions that are often asked about forgiveness:*
- Can a person forgive and still feel hurt?

- Does forgiving someone mean the person forgets what happened?
- Does refusal to go back into the situation that led to the offense mean the person has not forgiven?

►Can a person forgive and still hurt?

We cannot discuss forgiveness without talking about hurt because hurt is why there is a need to forgive. If someone does something to you and it does not hurt, you will have no need to forgive that person.

> *Being hurt or feeling the resulting pain from being wronged does not mean you are weak or unspiritual. You must admit that you hurt but should not feel guilty because you hurt.*

When we are hurt, the first thing we need to do is admit that we are hurt. Hurt is a natural response to an infraction done against us, so, being hurt or feeling the resulting pain from being wronged does not mean we are weak or unspiritual. We must admit that we hurt but should not feel guilty because we hurt. A lot of people confuse hurt with unforgiveness. That is a gross mistake.

> ➢ *Discuss the following vignette. In this vignette, could one confuse hurt with unforgiveness? If so how and why?*

Trudy has been married to her husband, Vincent, for ten years. Vincent is verbally abusive to her. Even though Trudy has gone out of her way to get his attention, he never affirms her or gives her compliments. His words to her are always humiliating and negative. Often when she tries to talk to him, he is doing something like texting or watching TV and is obviously not listening to her. Each time Trudy tries to share her concerns with Vincent — for example, things she experienced at work or church — he denounces her. In his eyes, she is always at fault. On several occasions, Trudy has expressed her concern about how Vincent relates to her, and each time he has apologized profusely. Trudy knows she needs to forgive him, so by God's grace, whenever Vincent apologizes, she accepts his apology. This is usually followed by a close and open conversation — the type of conversation Trudy desires — and Vincent's resolve to move forward and do better. But in a short while, Vincent always goes back to his old behavior. Eventually, Trudy decided it is not fair to continuously expose herself to such damaging experiences and started to withhold her thoughts and not share anything with Vincent. The home environment is now very static and tense.

Conversations are at the bare minimum and only as necessary. Vincent is now upset and accuses Trudy of not forgiving him because she is not talking to him.

6. Is Trudy hurt or unforgiving? Why? **She is hurt. Clearly, she is disappointed with how Vincent treats her. That is why she is protecting herself from further hurt.**

7. If she is unforgiving, what evidence do you see to make you come to this conclusion? **I don't think she is unforgiving. She forgave him many times. She saw no change, so she decided to protect herself from further hurt.**

8. Describe why Vincent may think Trudy has not forgiven him. **She's no longer talking to him, and it's safe to assume that the relationship is not getting better.**

9. If she is hurt, what evidence do you see to make you come to this conclusion? **Vincent's behavior had been going on for so long that eventually, Trudy decided it is not fair to continuously expose herself to such damaging experiences.**

10. If Trudy is hurt, does she have good reason to be hurt? **Yes. Her husband is treating her unfairly**.

11. Does Trudy's behavior help the situation? **No. Silent treatment does not foster a healthy relationship. Protecting herself from further hurt builds distance between them.**

12. Is Trudy's behavior damaging to her or her husband or her marriage? Could it be damaging to her relationship with her husband? **Trudy's behavior is damaging to her relationship. It's also damaging to her because her focus is solely on herself. While she does have a right to feel hurt, her behavior is not helping her relationship. Being hurt is okay — it's a natural reaction to what's being done to her — but how she's handling the hurt is the issue**.

13. How else could Trudy behave, or what else could she do to help the situation? **Trudy could come to the realization that she cannot change or control her husband's behavior, but she can control her own response to what he does. She can lower her expectation. She also could seek godly counsel and pray diligently about the matter. She could focus less on the hurt she is experiencing and focus on the relationship and the help her husband needs.**

> *No matter how bad the situation, you must come out a better person. You must come through whole, not broken.*

Although it is okay to hurt, there is potential danger in being hurt. When you hurt, you must quickly get low before God. Cry out to Him and allow Him to bring healing and comfort into your situation. You must not harbor the hurt. Once you recognize that hurt is there, run to the Great Physician. Seek His help. Do not keep replaying the situation in your mind. Do not brood over the injustice that was done to you.

Instead, think about how damaging this could be to you if you do not recover from it as quickly as possible. Do all you can with the power of the Holy Spirit that is in you to break free from the grip that hurt has on you and pursue your healing.

The objective is healing. No matter how bad the situation is, you must come out a better person. You must come through whole, not broken. To do this, you cannot linger in a place of hurt. Deal with it and consciously pursue your healing. The longer you stay hurt, the more likely it is for you to become offended.

▶ If hurt is okay, when does it become destructive?

> *When you forgive your offender, your loving heavenly Father, your healer heals you of the brokenness caused by the infraction. Forgiveness heals the hurt. So, forgiveness God's way brings restoration to the offended. Therefore, the person who has forgiven should no longer feel hurt.*

Refer to figure 2 on page 4. The process of unforgiveness indicates that hurt comes after an infraction, but if forgiveness does not occur in the early stages of the process, unforgiveness (a state of anger due to unfulfilled revenge) will set in, which, if not addressed, will ultimately lead to bitterness.

Therefore, a direct answer to the question — *Can one forgive and still feel hurt?* — is no. Hurt is natural, so we will hurt. But we must understand that we cannot forgive and still hurt. How so?

If you believe you have forgiven but you are still hurt, hurt is there not only because of the infraction against you, but because of how you recall the incident and the emotions that surface when the incident is recalled. First, when you forgive God's way, you write off the offense as if it never happened; it is rendered as nonexistent, so there should be no hurt. This does not mean that the hurtful incident is not a part of your past. Neither does it mean you get amnesia pertaining to the incident.

Writing off the incident and rendering it nonexistent means the negative meaning and emotions that are associated with this experience no longer exist. Therefore, when it comes back to memory, your response is not one of hurt, pain, anger, or any other negative emotions. If you still hurt upon recalling the incident, it is apparent that you have not written it off. So, you cannot forgive or write off (let go of) an incident and still hurt because of it.

Second, forgiveness is first a gift to the offended, then to the offender. When you forgive your offender, your loving heavenly

Father, your healer heals you of the brokenness caused by the infraction. Forgiveness heals hurt. So, forgiveness God's way brings restoration to the offended. Therefore, the person who has forgiven should no longer feel hurt.

9. Discuss how the following scriptures can help us deal with hurt and embrace forgiveness.

a. Romans 5:3-5— **Situations that cause us to hurt can produce endurance, patience, character, and hope. So, we should not go through them with complaints. We should see the glory (the benefit) in them**.

b. Hebrews 12:15— **We are warned against allowing bitterness in our hearts. Hurt is the seed to bitterness. Hurt yields unforgiveness, and unforgiveness yields bitterness, so it starts with hurt**.

10. What can we learn from David in Psalm 55? — **We should always turn to the Lord. Be honest with the Lord about how you feel. Hand the issue over to him. It is perfectly fine to describe your pain to Him. He understands. Let Him fight your battles. We should lift our heads, souls, eyes, and voices to Him in prayer.**

> See to it that no one falls short of the grace of God and that no bitter root grows up to cause trouble and defile many.
> —Hebrews 12:15, KJV

▶ Does forgiving someone mean you forget what happened?

Forgiving someone does not mean you get amnesia about what happened. You still remember what happened, but you do not remember the fine details. Also, when you do recall the incident, it is accompanied by a different set of emotions than those you felt before you forgave.

➢ *Discuss the following vignette.*

Michael is the pastor of a local church. One of his beloved nephews, James, serves on the ministerial staff. He has adopted James as a son and has mentored him over the years. Michael has given James many opportunities to serve in ministry, which resulted in James growing noticeably in the Lord. Their joint efforts, by the grace of God, have evolved into a thriving ministry; membership is growing, and the ministry is effective. James is clearly anointed. The hand of God is upon him. Whatever he does in ministry has had a positive impact on the people. Over time, however, James begins to think that he is not recognized enough and that he should have more authority and leadership in the ministry. So, he decides to start a church of his own. To Michael's surprise, more than half his membership leaves with his nephew because James actively recruited members from his uncle's church.

11. It is fair to say that Michael will think about what happened. While he is still hurting, in 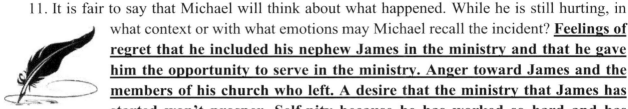 what context or with what emotions may Michael recall the incident? **Feelings of regret that he included his nephew James in the ministry and that he gave him the opportunity to serve in the ministry. Anger toward James and the members of his church who left. A desire that the ministry that James has started won't prosper. Self-pity because he has worked so hard and has suffered such setbacks**.

12. Give examples of behaviors towards James that could accompany Michael's recollection of the incident that would indicate that he has forgiven his nephew James. **Thanks to God that he had the opportunity to pour into James's life. Knowing that tribulation worketh patience (Romans 5:3); tears of joy that he was able to endure such a test.**

Forgiveness comes with a host of benefits to the offended. Forgiveness heals our wounded spirits and emotions. During the healing process, God erases the details of these painful events. This is yet another reason we cannot forgive and hurt at the same time. With healing comes a fresh outlook on the incident and the offender. God transforms our minds; therefore, our perception of the people and the circumstances are brought in alignment with His perfect will. As a result, we do not forget that something happened, but the way we recall the incident is unlike one that has been hurt.

Another reason you do not remember the details of the incident is because you have not been rehearsing it to yourself or to others.

13. Identify some dangers of rehearsing, retelling, replaying, or rethinking a hurtful experience. **Rehearsing, retelling, replaying, or rethinking the incident will only keep you stuck in that place of death**.

14. How can the following scriptures help the healing process after being hurt?

a. Exodus 14:14— **Be still and let the Lord fight for you. This will give you peace and will certainly help with the healing process.**

b. Romans 12:19— **Recognize that if you leave everything in God's hands, He will fight for you. He will avenge for you if you stay silent and still and let Him handle the situation.**

> The Lord shall fight for you, and ye shall hold your peace.
> —Exodus 14:14 (KJV)
>
> But without faith it is impossible to please him: for he that cometh to God must believe that he is, and that he is a rewarder of them that diligently seek him.
> —Hebrews 11:6 (KJV)

c. Philippians 4:8— **Instead of thinking about the bad that happened, think about the situation differently. Some possibilities: it could have been worse; you had good times with the person who hurt you; there are virtues you can learn from the experience; and you can gain strength and healing from meditating on God's words that address your situation.**

d. Hebrews 11:6— **Have the faith to believe all will be well and you will please the Lord.**

e. Romans 8:28— **As impossible as it seems, this will work out for your good as well. The verse says, "all things" and all means all.**

▶Does refusal to go back into the situation that led to the offense mean you have not forgiven?

It is instinctive for us to protect ourselves from pain and hurt. Consequently, the natural man would stay clear of interacting with someone who has done him harm. However, when you have written off something, and God has given you a new outlook, you do not see the person or situation from a natural perspective but through the lenses of a renewed mind, the mind of Christ. Going back into the same situation then becomes easy to do because it is as if the incident never happened.

A first fruit of forgiveness is the willingness to go back into the same situation that led to you being hurt. But the answer to this question is not a simple "Yes" or "No" because it depends on the situation. This may sound contradictory, so let us look at a couple of scenarios:

Vignette A: Audrey has served as the head of the worship ministry in her church for several years. The ministry is thriving, but unknown to her, David, a member of her church, is envious and wants to be in the position. He has set out to slander her with the hope that the pastors will remove her from the position, and he got his desire. Audrey was eventually removed from being the head of the worship ministry, and he was placed in the position. Over time, however, the worship ministry began to decline. It became apparent that David was not anointed for worship ministry; that he was not suitable for the position. The pastors asked Audrey to resume the position as worship leader but to keep David on the worship team.

- *Should Audrey take the position? Why? Why not?*
- *If she takes the position, should she do so on the condition that David does not serve on the worship team? Why? Why not?*

- *If Audrey has forgiven God's way, what would her response to the pastors' request look like?*

Vignette B: Twenty-three-year-old Kathy is friends with a small group of girls with whom she attended high school. She feels like she is least in the group and that she does not know as much as they know, and the girls treat her as such. They sometimes deliberately leave her out of things they are doing, they talk down to her, they whisper to each other about her in her presence, and they often insult her. This is an ongoing thing, and Kathy feels bad about herself. Many times, she leaves their presence feeling hurt. On occasion she has timidly expressed her feelings to the girls, but they simply laugh it off. There does not seem to be any indication from them that they are going to change.

- *Should Kathy maintain her friendship or association with these young ladies? Why? Why not? If not, what should she do?*
- *If Kathy decides to stay in touch with them but not as closely as before, does that mean she has not forgiven God's way? Why may (or may not) this decision be good for her?*
- *If Kathy has forgiven God's way, what would her behavior look like?*

---

15. In which vignette — A or B — should the offended be willing to go back into the situation if she has forgiven? Why? Why would it be best not to go back into one scenario or the other?

 **Scenario A. Ministry is not about us; it's about serving God with our whole heart. When we serve in ministry, we should expect to pay a price. There's no limit on the price we have to pay. It could cost us our reputations, our images, even our lives. It would be totally self-centered to see the ministry deteriorating, know you have the calling and the gift to effectively work the ministry, and decline rebuilding it because you are protecting yourself from hurt.**

I would not suggest going back to scenario B because this is an assault on who the person is, and it is ongoing. There is no evidence that things are going to change for the better. This situation can cause ruin to the inner person. Kathy leaves her "friends" feeling bad about herself each time. We must remember that we are the temple of the Holy Spirit (1 Corinthians 3:16); therefore, emotional and spiritual health is essential. We must provide a secure and clean place for the Holy Spirit to reside. An unhealthy or toxic relationship or environment is not good for her.

16. How should Kathy handle the situation if she decides not to make herself susceptible to the hurts of her "friends"?

She can create a safe distance between her and the girls. She doesn't have to cut them off completely, but she can create such a distance between her and them that they no longer have direct access or liberty to hurt her as before. For example, maybe she needs to stop going out with them or simply stop socializing with them. She can stay connected with them by some other means — maybe a quick phone call or text periodically.

17. Describe another situation that would be better not to go back into after being hurt. Why does this situation qualify as one that is not worth going back into? How would you handle this situation?

18. Describe another situation where a first fruit of forgiveness would be the return of the person who was offended to the situation that caused the hurt in the first place. Why does this situation qualify as one that is worth going back into?

Depending on the situation (as discussed earlier), refusal to place yourself at risk for a repeated infraction is a clear indication that you are still negatively affected by the past. This indicates that trust (at least on your part) is not restored.

Forgiveness comes with the ability to trust again, so without evidence of this, it is questionable if you have forgiven your offender.

The answer to this question is not a clear "Yes" or "No;" it depends on the circumstance. If, for example, the situation is repeated abuse, and the wrongdoer has not changed or has no desire to change, it would be self-destructing to return to such a situation, whether you have forgiven the perpetrator or not. Therefore, in circumstances where there is imminent danger or when the situation is unhealthy, be it physical, spiritual, or emotional, we can forgive the offender, but for our own well-being, it would not be wise to put ourselves back in those situations.

End the session with prayer. Suggested prayer points:

1. Healing from any lingering hurt.

2. Grace to deal with hurt in a healthy manner.

3. Grace to forgive God's way; to write off offenses against you as if they never happened.

Reflection and Personal Application

Give careful thought to how you've treated those who have offended you in the past and consider whether you have forgiven God's way. Based on what you just learned, write down what you customarily do and do not do God's way when dealing with hurtful situations. For example, when someone hurts you, do you find it difficult to get past the hurt? Do you rehearse the situation mentally or with anyone who will listen? Do you say you forgive the person, but you remind them of what they did to you?

As you identify the things you do when handling offense that are not in accordance with God's plan, write them down. Following that, write down the alternative that you can do to come in compliance with God's way of forgiving. Pray that God will give you the grace and humility to forgive His way.

> Forgiveness is a gift of love and is liberating. It liberates the offended first and then the offender.

Session Goal

By the end of this session, participants will

- know what forgiveness God's way looks like and
- address a few poignant questions about forgiveness.

What Is Forgiveness?

Discuss the following questions that are often asked about forgiveness:

► What if my offender is dead? Can I still forgive the person?

► Do I have to be friends with the person because I have forgiven him or her?

► If I forgive someone and never tell them, is that really forgiveness?

► What if the person is argumentative and won't accept forgiveness? Should I still forgive him or her?

► What if my offender is dead? Can I still forgive the person?

> *Ultimately, the purpose of forgiveness is first to free the offended and second to free the offender because the offended is bound by unforgiveness, not the offender.*

This question may sound odd to some people…Why would someone want to rectify a wrong done to them by someone who has already died? This is because forgiveness is for the benefit of the offended first, then for the offender. Unforgiveness is a prison that is built by the offended, and the person who is behind bars is the offended, not the offender. So, it is the offended that needs freedom, not the offender and forgiveness is what will set the offended free from this prison. The offender might have died, but if the situation was not resolved before the offender died, the offended still needs to be set free.

A couple of common circumstances in which this question is often asked are cases of domestic violence and sexual abuse. These offenses hurt deeply. Victims of these offenses often want restitution. As a result, the passing of the offender before there is restitution or any form of resolution only deepens the wound.

At first, it may seem unlikely to forgive the deceased, but it is quite doable and is just as much a mandate as it is for the living. So, the answer to this question is "Yes," one can forgive a person who is deceased.

Whether or not the offender is alive, your objective is to free yourself. You do not have the liberty to talk to or send a deceased person a letter or email, but again, the goal is to free yourself. So, your best option is to cancel the debt. Write it off. But how do you do this?

The following are possible options to forgive an offender who is deceased:

- Pretend the offender is sitting in an empty chair and have the "forgiveness talk" with them as if they are there.

- Write the offender the "forgiveness letter" as if they will read it.

- Write a detailed account of what happened as if you are telling the offender how you are affected by what they did. Include in the documentation how you want to bring the saga to a close.

1. Listed below are a few possible rationales offended individuals may use to explain why they think they will not be able to forgive a deceased person. Discuss each one. What advice or counsel would you give the offended person to change their perspective?

    a. Because the person is deceased, I cannot bring closure to the issue.

   It doesn't take both parties to bring closure to the issue. Forgiveness is a matter of the will. The offended simply needs the will, through the help of the Holy Spirit, to write off the debt. In the mind of the person who has forgiven, the offensive act never happened. That will bring it to closure.

    b. The person will never be able to apologize.

   This may be hard for the offended to accept, but forgiveness done God's way does not require an apology from the offender. So, if the offended is waiting for an apology for an offense against him or her that was carried out by a deceased individual, he or she will be offended forever. With this mindset, the offended will never experience the freedom that forgiveness offers.

    c. The person is deceased, so now that person has gotten away with what he or she has done to me. (This is particularly true for victims of sexual abuse.)

   People who feel this way often need to do write an account of what happened, describing how the offense has impacted them and how they want to bring things to closure, followed by a step-by-step discussion of the contents of the account. Usually,

it's easier to have the "forgiveness talk" or write the "forgiveness letter" after the discussion.

▶ Do I have to be friends with the person because I have forgiven him or her?

> *Reconciliation is the cessation of all ill feelings. It is a sure way to bring the saga to closure. It is resolution or settlement of the matter.*

Forgiveness is not the optimal outcome that God wants us to accomplish after an offense. He really wants us to reconcile with our offender. Reconciliation sets the stage and, in many cases, assures the restoration of trust and friendship. Many people find it so difficult to forgive that reconciliation becomes entirely unrealistic. But God's desire is that the broken relationship will be restored. That means if you were friends before, your friendship can be restored. If you were not friends before — although through the work of the Holy Spirit, the very opposite could happen — there's no expectation for the offender and offended who were not friends before an infraction to become

friends afterward. However, at a minimum, after forgiveness, the relationship should be restored to its original state. You might not be friends, but there should be absolutely no friction between you and the individual.

Keep in mind that if you were friends before, the relationship has been grossly compromised because of the infraction. Trust has been violated, so without a submissive will and emotions that are yielded to God, it could take quite some time to rebuild the relationship. If we do not yield our stubborn will, it is highly likely that the relationship will not go back to what it was. But with the grace of God and submitted hearts, the relationship could even get better than its original state. This depends first on the extent to which the offended is willing to die to self and second on the extent to which the offender is willing to humble himself or herself to facilitate restoration.

2. List some reasons why people who have been offended and who say they have forgiven their offender may think they don't need to be friends with the person who hurt them.

➤ *Ask the participants to share possible reasons why an offended person may think this way and follow-up with the questions below.*

   a. Do these reasons justify not wanting to be friends with someone who has offended them?

   b. What could be right or wrong about these reasons?

   c. How can we apply Luke 17:3-4 to address this issue?

Based on this scripture, address the issue with your offender. If the person apologizes, forgive him or her. That is grounds for friendship. If it's a case where the offender has the opportunity to repeatedly offend you, still forgive them.

▶ If I forgive someone and never tell that person, is that really forgiveness?

Forgiveness is liberating. It liberates you, as the offended, first, and then the offender. Therefore, if you have access to the offender and can directly extend forgiveness, you should do it. However, if you know the offender is not ready or willing to accept responsibility for their actions and realize that they need to be forgiven, it may be best to focus on freeing yourself and move on.

When you extend or convey forgiveness to your offender, you are telling the person that they committed an infraction against you, and you are forgiving them. For the person to accept forgiveness, they must admit to having done something hurtful to you.

Some people are not ready for this, and these are the ones you should consider forgiving without having an exchange with them. However, after forgiving the offender, whether you tell the person or not, your actions toward them should be genuinely loving and friendly. Your actions should be sufficient to tell them that you are at peace with them.

3. Give examples of circumstances in which it may be best not to tell the person you have forgiven them.

   a. **The person is likely to be argumentative**.

   b. **The person may attempt to rehearse the incident and place blame**.

   c. **The person is in denial about what he or she did**.

   d. **The person belittles your feelings. He or she thinks you're overreacting**.

4. What wrong had Jacob done to Esau? Read Genesis 27:1-30. **Jacob took advantage of Esau at a weak moment and robbed him of his birthright.**

5. Was Esau concerned about any of the scenarios listed under question 3? What evidence do you have for your answer? Read Genesis 33:3-4.

> [3] And he passed over before them, and bowed himself to the ground seven times, until he came near to his brother. [4] And Esau ran to meet him, and embraced him, and fell on his neck, and kissed him: and they wept.
> —Genesis 33:3-4, KJV

Despite these potential situations, if the offender is within reach, at least one attempt should be made to communicate to the individual that your intent is to move on from what has occurred. Also, if you are in prayer about the matter and have turned everything over to God, you should be careful to follow His lead.

By not talking to the offender, you could be limiting the ways in which God could bring complete healing to the situation. It is highly recommended that you try to the fullest extent.

Talk to the offender at least once, even if you suspect that they will not be receptive. If the person is not receptive, you will have done your part, and you can move on to free yourself and walk in forgiveness and the liberation that it brings.

►What if the person is argumentative and is unlikely to accept forgiveness? Should I still forgive him or her?

Absolutely! Forgiveness is not contingent upon the behavior of the offender. In fact, we should forgive our offenders whether they change their behavior or not.

> ➢ *Discuss the following scriptures regarding this statement: We should forgive our offenders whether they change their behavior or not.*

6.   What can we learn from the scriptures below about forgiveness?

a.   Luke 17:4— **Even if a person hurts us repeatedly, in a day, we should still forgive him or her**.

b. 1 John 4:9— **Christ loves us unconditionally, and we should endeavor to love in like manner. If we love this way, we will forgive, no matter what.**

c. 1 Corinthians 13:13— **Love is the greatest and a good way to show love is to forgive.**

> Even if they sin against you seven times in a day and seven times come back to you saying 'I repent,' you must forgive them."
> —Luke 17:4 (NIV)
>
> This is how God showed his love among us: He sent his one and only Son into the world that we might live through him.
> 1 John 4:9 (NIV)
>
> And now these three remain: faith, hope and love. But the greatest of these is love.
> 1 Corinthians 13:3 (NIV)

It is unfortunate that some people are not willing to admit to their wrongdoings and make amends. Instead, they become defensive and argumentative. But this should not stop you from forgiving even the most obstinate offender. You must still forgive the person, even if it means you must do so without having a face-to-face interaction with them.

> *Nothing short of forgiveness will suffice. We must try to the fullest extent to forgive.*

This is an exercise of wisdom because if, in your attempt to extend forgiveness, the offender becomes defensive and argumentative, tries to rehearse what happened, and places blame, it could make matters worse and take you down an unintended path. If that is the case, it is in your best interest to take the necessary steps to free yourself by letting the issue go with no expectations from the offender.

No matter how the offender conducts himself or herself, nothing short of forgiveness will suffice. We must try to the fullest extent to forgive. In fact, the ultimate is to go beyond forgiveness to reconciliation.

Reconciliation is the reunion of the offender and the offended. It calls for compromise on the part of both the offender and the offended. It means to come to an understanding. After reconciliation, the matter should never be revisited.

This means that when we say we forgive someone but still want nothing to do with that person, we have not really forgiven. We should forgive because we want to reconcile and settle the matter. And if the matter is settled, the offender and the offended should be able to live together and interact with one another peaceably.

Another Look at Forgiveness

This may sound conflicting but think about it, we all have the free will to choose, so forgiveness is a choice. But as children of God, people whose utmost desire should be to be like Jesus, we really have no choice. Yet many of us make the self-destructing decision not to forgive.

Forgiveness is an act of the will. Forgiveness is rooted in our love for our heavenly Father. If we confess that we love Him, we should demonstrate it through our acts of obedience to Him. It begins with a desire to please God, a desire to be that living sacrifice that apostle Paul spoke of in Romans 12:1.

7. How can we present our bodies as a living sacrifice? Discuss the following scriptures to answer this question.

> Therefore do not let sin reign in your mortal body so that you obey its evil desires. [13] Do not offer any part of yourself to sin as an instrument of wickedness, but rather offer yourselves to God as those who have been brought from death to life; and offer every part of yourself to him as an instrument of righteousness.
> —Romans 6:12-13 (NIV)

    a.   Philippians 2:12b-13— **In order to present our bodies as a living sacrifice, holy and pleasing to God, we must allow God's good and perfect will to be carried out in us**.

    b. 1 Peter 2:5— **We are a spiritual house, a holy priesthood, offering spiritual sacrifices that are acceptable to God. A perfect example of spiritual sacrifice is obedience to God when it would be easier and more favorable to our self-interest if we do things our way. An example of such obedience is the act of forgiveness.**

    c. Romans 6:12-13— **We should not let sin linger in us because if we do, we'll give in to evil desires. We should offer, submit, yield, and give ourselves to God and not to sin**.

    d. Romans 8:11-13— **We should not yield to the desires of the flesh. We should crucify the misdeeds of the flesh.**

If it were left up to us, we would never forgive because we hurt, and our instinctive response to pain or anything threatening or dangerous is fight or flight. Without God in our lives, without God's good purpose being fulfilled in us, when others hurt us, we would either seek revenge, defend, and protect ourselves (fight) or run away from the situation to prevent further harm (flight).

Neither fight nor flight constitutes forgiveness. Therefore, it is fair to say that forgiveness is not natural. It is completely against our nature to forgive someone who has hurt us. We cannot do this in our own strength. We need the help of the Holy Spirit to forgive.

Rationalizations Will Not Work

Many of us have an erroneous notion of what forgiveness really is. We allow excuses and selfish rationalizations to keep us in a subtle state of unforgiveness. But not even the most subtle state of unforgiveness is acceptable to God. He demands forgiveness His way, nothing less.

Following are a few of the rationalizations that keep us in a subtle but unacceptable state of unforgiveness:

> "You have heard that it was said, 'Love your neighbor and hate your enemy.' But I tell you, love your enemies and pray for those who persecute you, that you may be children of your Father in heaven. He causes his sun to rise on the evil and the good, and sends rain on the righteous and the unrighteous. If you love those who love you, what reward will you get? Are not even the tax collectors doing that? And if you greet only your own people, what are you doing more than others? Do not even pagans do that? Be perfect, therefore, as your heavenly Father is perfect.
> —Matthew 5:43-48

▶ I've forgiven them. I just don't have anything to do with them. It's like they don't exist.

Forgiveness brings about restoration. It restores relationships, our peace, our health, and, most of all, our spiritual well-being. Forgiveness is founded in love, so a statement such as this does not reflect the love of Christ. It is uncharacteristic of the love of Christ to have such an uncaring attitude toward a brother or sister. It is unforgiveness, not love, that will keep a person in this place.

8. Discuss how Matthew 5:43-48 addresses this perspective.

Suggestion: Read this Scripture in *The Message* Bible as well.

a. If we want to be children of our Father in heaven, what should we do? (Matthew 5:44-45).

We should love our enemies and pray for those who persecute us.

b. What is Matthew 5:45 saying?

Our Father in heaven causes the sun to rise upon the evil and the good — those who love Him and those who don't. We are to be like our heavenly Father if we are His children. We must love everyone — the evil and the good.

c.   What are verses 46 and 47 saying?

There is no reward in loving the people who love us. God does not regard that because even dishonest people, like tax collectors, do that, so big deal! Similarly, if we only talk to the people who talk to us, we're not doing anything more than anyone else. But we're not called to be like everyone else; we are called to be like Christ.

d.   Read Matthew 5:48 in *The Message* Bible. What does it say?

People who say they've forgiven but treat the person who offended them as if the person doesn't exist and choose not to have anything to do with that person need to grow up in Christ. They need to act like their heavenly Father. It is very uncharacteristic of our Father to write off someone and render them as nonexistent, so this crutch does not work.

►Every time I see the person who hurt me, I remember the injustice that was done to me.

People in this position are reliving the negative incident. They will relive a hurtful situation only because they have not let it go. To them, the incident happened, and it is not resolved. For these people, it is almost certain that when they recall the hurtful incident, it is accompanied by negative emotions. This is clear evidence that forgiveness has not taken place.

When we sin, we offend God, but when He sees us or when we call upon Him, He does not recall our offense against Him. So why should we recall the wrong done to us by others when we see them?

9.   Discuss how these scriptures address this perspective:

a.   Isaiah 43:25— **Jesus does not see our transgressions when He looks at us. We should endeavor to do the same with others.**

b.   2 Corinthians 12:9— **It may seem difficult to do what is stated in Isaiah 43:5, but here we are told that there is enough grace to enable us to do it. His grace is sufficient.**

> I, even I, am he who blots out your transgressions, for my own sake, and remembers your sins no more.
> —Isaiah 43:25 (NIV)
>
> But he said to me, "My grace is sufficient for you, for my power is made perfect in weakness." Therefore I will boast all the more gladly about my weaknesses, so that Christ's power may rest on me.
> 2 Corinthians 12:9 (NIV)

c. Hebrews 8:12 — **God forgives us of our sins, and He does not remember them**.

d. Psalm 103:12 — **Rather than treating us as we deserve, God removes our sins from us "as far as the east is from the west"—an immeasurable distance**.

►I've forgiven them, but I'm protecting myself from being hurt again. That's why I stay away from those who hurt me.

A person who takes this position does not trust. When you truly forgive, you trust again. When you forgive, trust is restored, along with the broken relationships that resulted from the infraction. The person who says this epitomizes the offended brother that Proverbs 18:19 talks about. This is the voice of an offended person. We cannot be offended and have forgiven at the same time.

> A brother offended is harder to be won than a strong city: and their contentions are like the bars of a castle.
> —Proverbs 18:19 (KJV)

10. Describe the offended in Proverbs 18:19.

a. **When we're offended, we build strong walls of protection around ourselves to avoid being hurt again. Also, we're contentious. It's difficult to win an offended person**.

b. **When there is an infraction and a brother (a person) is offended, it is very difficult to achieve reconciliation with them**.

c. **It is very difficult to get through to the offended. Their words are resistant. They are fortified like the bars of a city**.

Note, the term "fortified city" (often "fenced city" or "defended city" in the KJV) refers to a town with strong defenses, usually a massive wall structure and inner citadels or strongholds. (studylight.org)

End the session with prayer. Suggested prayer points:

1. That you would totally and entirely submit your will (your interest, your rights) to God so that the act of forgiveness does not seem impossible or too difficult to do.

2. That God would remove all excuses and all rationalizations that have given you cause not to forgive.

3. For a mind like Christ's — to see your brothers and sisters with the eyes of Christ, to hear your brothers and sister with the ears of Christ, and to be obedient to your heavenly Father as Christ was to the Father. He was obedient all the way to His death on the cross, and you must take up your cross and follow Him.

Reflection and Personal Application

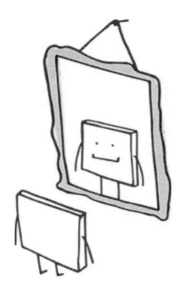

For this reflection I would like you to take a close look at Philippians 2:5. *"Let this mind be in you, which was also in Christ Jesus"* (KJV), or *"In your relationships with one another, have the same mindset as Christ Jesus"* (NIV).

Think about the mind of Christ. What characterizes His mind? Think about your mind. How does your mind differ from that of Christ? Pray that God will remove the differences and make your mind like His Son's mind. This may seem impossible, but it is not. If it were impossible, this verse would not be written in the Word of God.

Ask God to help you think, feel, and judge more and more like Christ. This process is governed by God's Holy Spirit, who teaches you the ways of Christ. One of the major ways the Spirit of God instructs and transforms you is through His Word. As you read, study, reflect upon, internalize, and obey the written Word of God, the Spirit is at work in you, and is helping you to have the mind of Christ. Second, you must be consistent in prayer to take on and maintain a mind like Christ's. Ask God to give you a desire for and discipline and delight in His Word and in prayer.

Unit 4: The Rewards of Forgiveness

Session 15: It's Blessed to Forgive

Forgiveness is an act of obedience to God, and God honors obedience. Unforgiveness, on the other hand, is a sin, and sin separates us from God.

Session Goal

By the end of this session, participants will learn about the blessings that are associated with forgiveness.

An Act of the Will

Forgiveness requires a determination to please God. It is an act of a submitted will. It is an act of obedience to God. Through submission, a yielded spirit, we must, with the help of the Holy Spirit, obey God and therefore forgive our offenders, even when our emotions tell us something else. Apostle Paul said in Romans 7:25, *"I thank God through Jesus Christ our Lord. So then with the mind I myself serve the law of God; but with the flesh the law of sin"* (KJV). The mind is one of the three parts of the soul, the other two parts being the will and emotions. All three must submit to God.

Apostle Paul is telling us that it is with a determined mind that he serves God. He also tells us in Romans 12:2 that to be transformed, our minds must be renewed. Therefore, we must allow the Word of God to change our way of thinking, which in turn will enable us to make up our minds to forgive. This transformation will bring our emotions, mind and will in line with God's will and ultimately to the act of forgiveness.

➢ *Discuss the following statements.*

1. Forgiveness is not an act based on emotions.

2. Forgiveness is an act of the will. It is the manifestation of a will and mind submitted and reformed by the Word of God.

Forgiveness God's Way

3. Is an apology necessary before the offended forgives? Use  Romans 5:8 as the basis of your answer. **The offender does not need to apologize or acknowledge he or she has wronged us. Christ made provision for the forgiving of our sins while we were sinning against Him and before we asked for forgiveness.**

> If it be possible, as much as lieth in you, live peaceably with all men.
> —Romans 12:18 (KJV)
>
> 23 "Therefore, if you are offering your gift at the altar and there remember that your brother or sister has something against you, 24 leave your gift there in front of the altar. First go and be reconciled to them; then come and offer your gift.
> —Matthew 5:23-24 (NIV)

The forgiving person walks away peacefully from the evil done to them, knowing that the offender may never accept responsibility for what they have done, let alone apologize. Refer to Romans 12:18 and Matthew 5:23-24.

4. What are the main points you learn from these scriptures?
   a. Romans 12:18— **The offended must try as much as possible to make peace with their offender.**
   b. Matthew 5:23-24— **The offended should take the initiative to make peace with the offender. Seek to reconcile with your offender before offering your gift to the Lord.**

When we forgive, we embrace the fact that the offender owes us nothing; not even an acknowledgement that they did us wrong. Therefore, we do not expect anything from the offender or anyone else to make us feel or look better.

The offended writes off the evil done to them like a debt that is pardoned. A debtor is not required to pay a debt that is pardoned. Likewise, an offender is not required to offer an apology for an offense that is written off.

5. What are the main points you learn from these scriptures?
   a. Matthew 18:26-27— **When the servant asked for time to repay him, the lord pitied him, canceled the debt, and let him go. The lord wrote off the debt. Our Lord and Savior responds to us similarly when we ask for pardon.**

   b. Micah 7:18-19— **God pardons sins and forgives transgressions. God does not stay angry forever. God delights in showing mercy. God will cast away our iniquities into the depths of the sea.**

When we forgive, it is as if the infraction against us never happened (Hebrews 8:12).

6. When we forgive, we do not recall the incident the same way we did when we had not forgiven. Does this mean we have amnesia? **No, God doesn't give us amnesia because we do recall that the incident happened. However, He graciously erases the details of the incident. The details cause pain. Although we know the incident occurred, through His love the Holy**

Spirit causes us not to remember the details. When God erases the details, the emotions that accompany the recollection of the incident are not negative or painful. Instead, they are emotions of praise and thanksgiving for victory over the plan of the enemy.

A first fruit of forgiveness is the willingness to go back into the situation that caused us hurt. This is circumstantial, however. There are situations that are sufficiently harmful, that makes it in our best interest to avoid those situations.

7.   Refer to 1 Corinthians 6:19. How can you use this Scripture to explain not going back into the situation that hurt you in the first place? **This tells me that if our bodies house the Holy Spirit, we should take very good care of it. In doing so, we should avoid situations that are damaging to us**.

> Do you not know that your bodies are temples of the Holy Spirit, who is in you, whom you have received from God? You are not your own;
> —1 Corinthians 6:19 (NIV)
>
> Jesus answered, "I tell you, not seven times, but seventy-seven times.
> —Matthew 18:22 (NIV)

8.   In addressing this point, does Matthew 18:22 support or contradict the point made by 1 Corinthians 6:19? **No, it does not contradict 1 Corinthians 6:19. You can forgive and not be back in that harmful/damaging and potentially dangerous situation. The condition of your heart towards the offender must be right, even though they would continue to hurt you**.

9.   Does breaking away from a situation that causes ongoing harm mean a person has not forgiven? **You can forgive the offender but carefully create a healthy distance between the offender and you, solely because you know fellowship with that individual is harmful**.

10. Discuss the scenario below. What can the niece do?

An aunt adopts an orphaned niece as a teenager. The aunt emotionally abuses the niece. She controls her, makes all the decisions for her, tells her what to do, and makes her feel like she is not capable of doing anything much. The niece feels like her aunt totally dismisses her feelings. This is robbing her of the opportunity to grow and develop as an independent and confident young woman and the niece is getting increasingly angry at her aunt, especially when she sees her peers doing things that she could never dream of doing. But one looking in from the outside would not readily see the aunt's destructive behavior. The niece's material needs are adequately met, and she is very involved in youth ministry, thanks to the encouragement of her aunt. It is apparent though, that the aunt intends to continue this pattern of behavior, even beyond the niece's teenage years.

___

Possible Answer: It may be best for the niece to separate herself physically from the aunt as soon as she is able to do so. She can forgive the aunt but maintain a relationship with the aunt from a safe distance. There should be sufficient distance in her relationship with her aunt so that the aunt does not have the footing to degrade or control her niece.

___

Numerous rewards await us when we forgive.

- Enriched relationship with our Father.
- Enriched relationships with others.
- Positions us to be used by God.
- Emotional healing.
- Makes us better not bitter.
- Physical healing.

▶ Enriched Relationship with Our Father

Nothing is more rewarding than a right relationship with our Lord and Savior, Jesus Christ. Unforgiveness is a sin, and sin separates us from God. Forgiveness, on the other hand, is an act of obedience to God, and God honors obedience. There are numerous scripture references about God's take on obedience.

> Whatever you have learned or received or heard from me, or seen in me—put it into practice. And the God of peace will be with you.
> —Philippians 4:9
>
> Now if you obey me fully and keep my covenant, then out of all nations you will be my treasured possession. Although the whole earth is mine,
> —Exodus 19:5
>
> Keep this Book of the Law always on your lips; meditate on it day and night, so that you may be careful to do everything written in it. Then you will be prosperous and successful.
> —Joshua 1:8

11. From the following scriptures, identify how obedience can enrich our relationship with God.
   a. Philippians 4:9— **The God of peace will be with us**.
   b. Exodus 19:5— **We will be God's treasured possession, although the whole earth is His. We will be special to Him if we are obedient**.
   c. Joshua 1:8— **We will be prosperous and successful**.
   d. John 14:15— **Obedience is an expression of our love for God**.

We cannot forgive in God's way and not love God's way. Forgiveness and agape love go hand in hand. Jesus was hanging on the cross when He said, *"Father, forgive them, for they do not know what they do"* (Luke 23:34 KJV). Amid the gravest offense ever done to anyone who walked the earth, He forgave because He is love. We cannot forgive unless the love of God dwells in us. God is love, and with His love in us, as we act upon it, we are acting like Him.

▶ Enriched Relationship with Others

Next to a good relationship with our Maker, we need to maintain healthy relationships with others. To establish and maintain healthy relationships, we must be emotionally sound. This means we must be able to trust others. We cannot be suspicious, insecure, vengeful, overly sensitive, self-centered, or angry. These character flaws will ruin relationships. Unforgiveness clutters our spirits with all these things and more, making it most unlikely to maintain or even establish a healthy relationship with others.

Whether we forgive and walk in peace and love, or do not forgive and walk in bitterness, everything from within us will spill over into our relationships. Without debate, living under the blessings of forgiveness is much more honorable than the dark effects of unforgiveness.

When we forgive, we tell our Father, Satan, and anyone else who will listen that our interests in self-preservation are secondary to the will of God. In turn, God blesses us with His sweet, settled peace. This enables us to love ourselves and love others. This love will serve as the catalyst for healthy relationships with others.

12. Considering the following scriptures, how could forgiveness facilitate an enriched relationship with others?

    a.   Ephesians 4:2-3— **If we operate in love, we will be able to forgive and to be gentle and patient with others. This will facilitate peaceful relationships**.

    b.   John 15:13— **Denying yourself by forgoing retribution is synonymous to laying down your life**.

    c.   2 Corinthians 5:17-18— **We were all given the ministry of reconciliation**.

▶ Positions Us to Be Used by God

> *When we forgive, we are going deep in our spirits to pull out a sacrificial offering to God.*

God is looking to use fully dedicated and sold-out vessels. He will not share supremacy of our lives with anyone or anything else. He must be sole ruler and Lord over us. The act of forgiveness tells God that He is indeed the head of our lives. It tells Him that we are willing to sacrifice our own feelings and interests to promote His interests.

More important, it tells God that we will do anything, even what hurts us, to walk in obedience to Him. This is what God is looking for in His vessels.

When we forgive, we are telling God that He occupies the first and highest place in our lives. We are telling Him that we do not value our pride, our feelings, our image, or our interests above His desires toward us. God's interpretation of this is that we are available for His use.

Why am I placing so much emphasis on forgiveness when there are so many other ways that we can let God know He is first in our lives? I emphasize forgiveness because the act of forgiveness goes directly and entirely against the core of our beings. By nature, we all seek to protect ourselves, and most of us do so by any means necessary. Anger management specialist and author Lynette Hoy says, *"Human behavior suggests that people are hard-wired to retaliate when they have been hurt by another person."*[4]

A natural response when faced with potential hurt or danger is to defend ourselves. Therefore, when we forgive, we are going deep in our spirits to pull out a sacrificial offering to God. We now have laid our lives down at the expense of our pride, feelings, self-interest, and self-preservation, all for the glory of God. This positions us to be used by God.

13. What do the following scriptures say about our positioning ourselves to be used by God?

    a.   2 Timothy 2:21— **We must clean our vessels, purify ourselves**.

    b.   Colossians 4:2— **Devote ourselves to prayer, be watchful, and thankful**.

    c.   Revelation 3:3— **Hold on to what we've been taught, and repent**.

▶ Emotional Healing

> *Unforgivenes s keeps us bound, but forgiveness frees us.*

Unforgiveness keeps us in a dark place of mistrust, anger, and even depression. It leaves us emotionally sick. Sin itself is a weight, but one of the heaviest sins to carry around is unforgiveness. Unforgiveness keeps us bound, but forgiveness frees us. Forgiveness gives us peace. It takes the burden of sin off us. Forgiveness allows us to see our offender through the lenses of love.

When we forgive, we don't carry around this unpaid debt that we think is due to us. Forgiveness rids us of the desire for payback due to the wrong that happened to us.

A state of unhealthy expectancy can leave us angry. It can rob us of peaceful sleep, laughter, and joy. It most certainly hinders us from trusting others because unforgiving people are determined to ensure no one else ever hurts them again. On the other hand, forgiveness guarantees the complete opposite, making us considerably emotionally healthier.

We cannot separate the act of forgiveness from the love of God. It is only with a heart that is completely open to God that we can forgive. Likewise, it is only with a forgiving heart that we can love completely, and it is only those who are emotionally healthy that can truly love another.

Love and acts of kindness yield the same results. In the same way, loving and letting go require us to open our hearts and even take risks. Receiving the same from others requires that we open our hearts and take risks as well. An emotionally unhealthy person cannot trust sufficiently to open their heart to another and take risks. We must be emotionally sound to do so. Forgiveness, empowered by the love of God, is what gets us there.

▶ Makes Us Better, Not Bitter

> *Bitterness is not just a state of being angry. It is hardened anger or chronic resentment.*

According to figure 3 on page 4, bitterness is a potential result of being hurt by another. We become bitter when we do not forgive. Bitterness is not just a state of being angry. It is hardened anger or chronic resentment. It is prolonged anger, which has now become crystalized. Anger results from the unfulfilled desire for revenge. Therefore, if there's no revenge, the unforgiving person remains angry and will eventually become bitter.

This does not have to be the route we take. If we love God, we should know that *"all things work together for good to them that love God, to them who are the called according to his purpose."* (Romans 8:28 KJV).

We should realize that no matter how painful the situation, if we remove our self-interests, it will work for our good. The scripture says *all* things, not some or most things. The problem is, when situations arise, we often forget the Word, or we make the Word conditional; that

is, we believe the Word works or is applicable in some situations but not in others.

We may ask how an assault against an innocent person could work for their good. We must understand that God is paradoxical. He breaks us to mend us, empties us out to fill us. He puts us through the fire to purify us, tests us before rewarding us, and humbles us to exalt us. If we endure the humbling situations in which He places us, it tells us (not Him because He knows all things) that we are potentially ready to be exalted.

Similarly, if we can go through a hurtful situation at the hands of someone we least expect, that experience should tell us we are being equipped to do more than we were doing. Maybe, as a result, we will learn to truly love our enemies, or maybe the experience will make us better equipped to counsel someone who has been hurt. Our act of forgiveness could also open the door for God to elevate us in ministry and entrust more to our care because we have shown that our well-being does not come first. These outcomes would make us better, not bitter.

14. Talk about how the characters in any of the vignettes listed below could conduct themselves to make sure they come out better, not bitter? Discuss some things that the characters in the vignettes could do to show that they are better not bitter.
    a. Carol, nitpicking — page 20.
    b. Jerome, verbal abuse — page 22.
    c. Sarah, emotional neglect — page 23.
    d. Lisa, controlling parents — page 23.
    e. Sister ABC needed help from church — page 37.

f.   Samantha, sexually molested by father page 38.
g.   Mary, tumultuous marriage — page 52.
h.   Tracy, argument with twin sister — page 53.
i.   Denise, disrespected by choir director — page 64.
j.   Doris and Veronica, victims of domestic violence — page 87.
k.   Trudy, verbal abuse — page 93.
l.   Michael, church split — page 96.
m.   Kathy, treated badly by friends — page 99.
n.   Audrey, slandered by brother in Christ — page 98.
o.   The adopted, orphaned niece — page 116.

▶Physical Healing

Forgiveness is good for our hearts. One study from the *Journal of Behavioral Medicine* found forgiveness is associated with lower heart rate and blood pressure, as well as stress relief. This can bring long-term health benefits for our hearts and overall health.

Everett L. Worthington Jr. reports in the article "The New Science of Forgiveness" that a study found forgiveness is positively associated with five measures of health: physical symptoms, medications used, sleep quality, fatigue, and somatic complaints. This study's findings indicate that reduced negative effects, such as depressive symptoms, link to strengthened spirituality, conflict management, and stress relief that we find through forgiveness and that these all have a significant impact on our overall health.[5]

In another study, Charlotte vanOyen Witvliet, a psychologist at Hope College in Holland, Michigan, asked people to think about someone who had hurt, mistreated, or offended them. While they thought about this person and his or her past offense, Dr. Witvliet monitored their blood pressure, heart rates, facial muscle tension, and sweat gland activity.[6]

To think over past offensive experiences is like floundering in unforgiveness. Findings indicate that when people recalled a hurtful experience, their physiological responses, such as sweating, blood pressure, and heart-rate increase, corroborate this assertion. Thinking about their past hurtful experiences proved stressful, and the participants reported thinking over these experiences was not pleasant. It made them feel angry, sad, anxious, and less in control.

Witvliet also asked the participants to try to empathize with their offenders or imagine forgiving them. When they practiced forgiveness, their physiological arousals decreased. Essentially, they showed normal stress reaction when they practiced forgiveness.

To determine whether people's stress levels related to their ability to forgive a romantic partner, Worthington Jr. measured levels of cortisol in the saliva of thirty-nine people who rated their relationship as either terrific or terrible.

Cortisol is a hormone that metabolizes fat for quick response to stress (and, after the stress ends, redeposits the fat where it is easily accessible—around the waist). More people who reported poor (or recently failed) relationships tended to have higher baseline levels of cortisol, and they scored worse than their counterpart who did not report poor or failed relationships on a test that measures their general willingness to forgive.

Their stress hormone level increased—more cortisol reactivity—when asked to think about their relationships. Those increases in stress were highly correlated with their unforgiving attitudes toward their partners. People with very happy relationships were not without stresses and strains in their relationships. Even so, forgiving their partners' faults contributed to keeping their physical stress in the normal range.

In a study led by Loren Toussaint, along with David Williams, Marc Musick, and Susan Everson, a national survey asked nearly 1,500 Americans to indicate the degree to which each person practiced and experienced forgiveness (of others, of self, and even if they thought they had experienced forgiveness by God). Participants also reported on their physical and mental health. They found a significant relationship between forgiving others and

positive health among middle-aged and older Americans. People over forty-five years of age who had forgiven others reported greater satisfaction with their lives, and they were less likely to report symptoms of psychological distress, such as feelings of nervousness, restlessness, and sadness.[7]

Unforgiveness is associated with negative health symptoms because hostility is a central part of unforgiveness. Hostility has been found to be the part of type A behavior that seems to have the most malignant health effects, such as increased risk of cardiovascular disease. Forgiveness frees us from hostility and all its unhealthy consequences.

Hostility and stress probably aren't the only factors that link unforgiveness to poor physical health. According to a recent review of literature on forgiveness and health done by Worthington Jr. and Michael Scherer, unforgiveness might compromise the immune system at many levels. This review suggests that unforgiveness might throw off the production of important hormones and even disrupt the way our cells fight off infections, bacteria, and other physical ailments, such as mild periodontal disease.[8]

15. What do these scriptures say about sin/unforgiveness and physical illness?

    a.   John 9:1-2— **Physical illnesses are sometimes due to sin.**

    b.   Proverbs 12:25— **Anxiety, a heavy heart can weigh down one's spirit, which can result in physical illness.**

    c.   Proverbs 15:13— **Unforgiveness takes away your joy, which can result in physical illness.**

According to Dr. Michael Barry, over 61 percent of cancer patients have forgiveness issues. So, this issue is killing people—literally.

We can deal with personal infractions in many ways. We do not have to choose to forgive, but if we choose not to forgive, we will pay the price with our physical, mental, relational, and/or spiritual health. Research shows that forgiveness can be beneficial to our physical health.

End the session with prayer. Suggested prayer points:

1. Strength from the Holy Spirit to carry no grudge and forgive quickly when offended.

2. A will that is yielded entirely to God that will allow you to forgive, as defined by God, not you.

3. That you will see the benefits of forgiveness manifested in your life.

Reflection and Personal Application

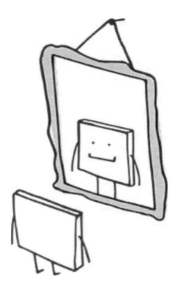

Think about how you respond when you've been offended. Do you forgive readily? Do you get deeply hurt? Do you get hurt, as the average person does, but can move on healthily in reasonably good time? When you forgive, how do you know you've truly forgiven? Do you forgive God's way, and if so, how do you know you've done so?

Think about a particular situation and how you handled the offense. Based on what you've learned so far, assess whether you handled the situation God's way or whether you've forgiven God's way. If you have, pray for God's grace to continue in His Word. If you have not, pray for help from the Holy Spirit to handle offensive situations as Christ would. Pray for a work of the Holy Spirit to be done in your heart so that you can forgive God's way. Pray for grace to hurt in a healthy manner when you get hurt.

Reconciliation is the signature on forgiveness that tells the offender that the debt is canceled, and the offended is moving on.

Session Goal

By the end of this session, participants will learn about

- the goal of forgiveness,
- the dynamics of reconciliation, and
- the difference between forgiveness and reconciliation.

Reconciliation

Forgiveness is good, but reconciliation is best. Reconciliation takes us beyond forgiveness. It clears the air and brings both parties to a place of compromise. Reconciliation moves the parties from opposing ends to the reinstatement of mutual respect and peace.

When responding to the mandate of our heavenly Father, we ought to do our best. Good is not good enough. When Jesus died for the forgiveness of our sins, His ultimate objective was our reconciliation back to our Father in heaven. Another word for reconciliation is union. Jesus's death on the cross earned humankind our reunion with God after sin severed a loving relationship with Him.

Reconciliation is one more essential element in carrying out the mandate to forgive. Another synonym for this term is compromise. For compromise to take place, both the offender and the offended must give in or rescind some grounds they have held in some way, shape, or form. This means that even the offended, the one who was hurt, is required to make some changes.

Without a doubt, forgiveness is a tall order. For many, it is too much to ask. However, keep in mind it cannot measure up to what God did for us, so He is not asking us to do anything He has not done. Even though forgiveness places such a demand on us, there is a more honorable step beyond forgiveness, and that is reconciliation.

1. **Forgiveness** is a conscious decision to pardon or **cancel** the debt that is owed due to the **infraction** done against the offended.

2. **Reconciliation** is to bring the offended and the **offender** together to restore **the relationship**.

3. One can forgive and there is no **reconciliation**, but there can be no reconciliation without **forgiveness**.

4. **Reconciliation** focuses on relationships and **resolution** focuses on the problem.

5. How do the following scripture passages confirm that reconciliation is a necessity?
   a. Romans 12:18— **As followers of Christ, one of our main objectives is to live in harmony with others. Romans 12:18 tells us that according to the power in us, we should endeavor to live peaceably with everyone. The sole act of forgiveness may or may not bring about reconciliation. In fact, it often does not. Most times, we need to take deliberate steps to ensure reconciliation.**
   b. 2 Corinthians 5:18— **God demonstrated reconciliation for us. He reconciled the world to Himself through Christ, and as a result, we are given the ministry of reconciliation. We are all called to the ministry of reconciliation.**
   c. Psalm 34:14b— **We must do something to restore peace. Peace will not find us; we must pursue it.**

> If it be possible, as much as lieth in you, live peaceably with all men.
> —Romans 12:18 (KJV)
>
> And all things are of God, who hath reconciled us to himself by Jesus Christ, and hath given to us the ministry of reconciliation;
> —2 Corinthians 5:18 (KJV)
>
> Depart from evil, and do good; seek peace, and pursue it.
> Psalm 34:14 (KJV)

Take the Extra Step

A face-to-face confrontation (not meant to be negative, as people often think) is often necessary for reconciliation. In this encounter, both parties should admit any problematic role they have played and give each other the benefit of the doubt. When you take the extra step of obedience and pursue reconciliation, it is not up to you to secure cooperation from those who offend you. If you take that extra step in the love of Christ, and your offenders are resistant, you are not at fault. Know that God is pleased with you.

By taking this step, you seal the act of forgiveness, whether your offenders cooperate or not. This should tell your offenders that you have forgiven them without reservation.

You should take advantage of every opportunity to facilitate reconciliation when needed. You should most definitely forgive, but if your offenders are accessible, you should take the next step to reconcile with them. Reconciliation will let your offenders know directly from you that you are ripping up the revenge bill, that you have written off the debt, and that they owe you nothing.

The benefits of such a gift are immeasurable to you and your offenders. First, it sets everyone free, and it tells the offenders that you are amenable to restoring your relationship with them. If nothing else, it brings relief and a sense of peace to everyone.

6. Who took the extra step toward reconciliation in the following scriptures?

a. Genesis 33:4, 10— **Both brothers. As these brothers were reconciled, so must we be reconciled with our brethren before we can hope to approach the Lord in sincerity**.

b. Genesis 45:1-7— **A moving testimony to the power of reconciled relationships is evidenced in Joseph's act of revealing himself to his brothers, treating them kindly, and forgiving them of the terrible things they had done to him**.

c. Genesis 50:15-20— **When Jacob, the father of the twelve brothers, died, Joseph's brothers feared that he would act out in revenge against them. They thought he was holding out until their father died. But Joseph wept and treated them with kindness because he was aware of God's sovereign purpose in what had happened**.

d. Luke 15:11-22— **The younger of two sons insolently rejected the love of his father and chose instead the company of his fast-living, fickle friends. The father's broken heart longed for the return of his wayward son. When he finally saw him coming in the distance, the father felt compassion for him, ran to him, embraced him, kissed him, and joyously welcomed him back into the family. That powerful story shows the tremendous joy, both of reconciled human relationships and of sinners being reconciled to our heavenly Father**.

> [4] But Esau ran to meet Jacob and embraced him; he threw his arms around his neck and kissed him. And they wept. [10] "No, please!" said Jacob. "If I have found favor in your eyes, accept this gift from me. For to see your face is like seeing the face of God, now that you have received me favorably.
> —Genesis 33:4, 10 (NIV)

Pray for Your Offenders

7. Discuss how Matthew 5:44 and Proverbs 10:12 facilitate reconciliation.

a. Matthew 5:44— **By praying sincerely for your offenders, you establish the atmosphere for reconciliation. We cannot pray sincerely for anyone we don't love. With love in place, reconciliation is bound to happen. Total submission to God, out of your love for your God, will enable you to pray for those who hurt you deeply and take the extra step beyond forgiveness to reconciliation**.

b. Proverbs 10:12— **As you pray for your offenders, and God fills your heart with love for them, this love will overshadow their offense against you, rendering it irrelevant. This will play a big part in your healing and your ability to go beyond forgiveness to reconciliation**.

> Hatred stirs up conflict, but love covers over all wrongs.
> —Proverbs 10:12

End the session with prayer. Suggested prayer points:

1. That with as much as is in you, you will actively seek and pursue peace.

2. That you will speak well of (bless with your words) your offenders.

3. That you will do kind deeds for your offenders.

4. That you will pray diligently and sincerely for your offenders.

5. For strength from the Holy Spirit to take the extra step to reconcile with anyone who has offended you.

Reflection and Personal Application

Read and meditate on Matthew 5:44 — *"But I say unto you, Love your enemies, bless them that curse you, do good to them that hate you, and pray for them which despitefully use you, and persecute you."*

I call this verse the antidote for unforgiveness. If nothing else works, this does. The action words in this very important verse are love, bless, do good (be kind), and pray.

If you're in the midst of a situation where you need to forgive an offender, write down at least one thing you can do to show love to your offender, to bless your offender, and to do good to your offender, and after writing these things down, pray for your offender.

> With the help of the Holy Spirit, the seemingly impossible mandate to forgive is well within our reach.

Session Goal

By the end of this session, participants will

- be reminded that the strength to obey the mandate to forgive is within them and
- learn practical steps to come in alignment with God's mandate to forgive.

Greater Is He Who Is in You

Based on the extent to which unforgiveness pervades the Church, one would think the command from God to forgive is unreasonable and cannot be attained. This is a strong delusion from Satan. It is reasonable for God to require that we forgive those who offend us, and it is for our own good, not His. The mandate to forgive is well within our reach with the help of the Holy Spirit. No matter how seemingly difficult and painful it is, we can forgive because *"the one who is in you is greater than the one who is in the world"* (1 John 4:4b, NIV). Our humble response to the command of our Father should be the act of forgiveness, but too many of us find it difficult to do so.

God has not revoked our free will to choose. Therefore, from a carnal perspective, we can choose to forgive or not to forgive, but as followers of Christ, we really have no choice but to forgive. This is a mandate from God, our Father. A mandate is a command, and commands are not up for debate or negotiation, especially when they come from the Sovereign One.

God sent His Son Jesus to die for our sins so that we may be reconciled to Him. Romans 5:8 says, *"God demonstrated his own love for us in this: While we were still sinners, Christ died for us."* He laid down His life for us while we were sinners and before we even knew we needed forgiveness, let alone asked Him for forgiveness. After doing this much for us, all He asks is that we forgive others as He has forgiven us, and none of us will ever have to die an ignominious death such as the one He endured to forgive us. So, even so, we are not going the length He did to forgive us.

God is looking for obedience. He wants self-sacrificing obedience. But given the state of the Church, it appears as if this command is unrealistic. This is a lie from the enemy that many in the Church seem to believe.

Submit Yourself to God

The demand to forgive in the face of injustice brings us to the end of our own capabilities; it requires spiritual strength.

1. Jesus seems to have gotten to the end of His strength before He went to the cross. Refer to Matthew 26:36-46.

    a. What did He do to fall in line with the command of His Father? Refer to verse 36. **He prayed**

    b. How many times did Jesus pray about the matter? Refer to verses 36, 42, and 44. **Three**

    c. What emotions was Jesus feeling? Refer to verses 37 and 38. **Exceedingly sorrowful, troubled, heavy in His spirit**.

    d. In addition to praying, what did Jesus do to fall in line with the command of His Father? Refer to verse 49. **He gave up / yielded His will to the will of His Father…not what I want, but what You want**.

    e. How did His Father respond to Him? **God sent an angel to strengthen Him**.

    f. At what point did the response come? Refer to Luke 22:42-43. **Right after He surrendered His will. Immediately after He said "nevertheless, not as I will, but as you will."**

    > [42] "Father, if you are willing, take this cup from me; yet not my will, but yours be done." [43] An angel from heaven appeared to him and strengthened him.
    > —Luke 22:42-43 (NIV)

2. What lessons can we learn from Jesus when we feel we do not have the strength to do what our heavenly Father asks us to do? **Pray and surrender our will to Him**.

3. What does James 4:7 say regarding the question above? **Again, our paradoxical God asks us to do the opposite of what we need to obtain what we need. To gain strength, we must become weak or admit to Him that we are indeed weak. In doing so, we must submit, surrender, and yield ourselves to Him. We must be weak so that His strength can overrule our strength. After coming under His strength, we will be able to resist the devil or resist the temptation to hold on to unforgiveness, and it will flee from us**.

4. What does James 4:7 look like when put into action? **A submitted life has no self-interest. The priority for a submitted life is pleasing God at all costs. A submitted life embraces the fact that we have no rights, not even to defend ourselves when we've done no wrong. A fruit of the life of a submitted individual is meekness**.

5. What assurance do we have that we have the strength to do what the Father asks us to do?

   a. 2 Timothy 1:14— **The Holy Spirit lives in us**.

   b. 1 John 4:4— **The One who lives in us is greater than the one in the world**.

   c. 2 Corinthians 12:9— **God's grace is enough to empower us to obey Him and when we are too weak to obey, He becomes strong and His power rests on us**.

6. The Holy Spirit is our **Paraclete**. The word "paraclete" comes from the Greek word *parakletos*, which means "**Comforter**" or "**Counselor**" or "one called to the side of another."

7. What does John 14:16 tell us the Holy Spirit will do for us? **He will be an advocate (supporter) to help us and be with us forever**.

➤ *Discuss. "So, do you think you have enough help to forgive?"*

8. What is meekness? **Meekness is restrained power. It is the act of making a conscious decision not to defend one's own rights. A meek person has a disciplined and controlled spirit.**

9. Given the definition of meekness, how does it play a role in forgiveness? **Because of submission to God, when the meek are wronged, they do not exercise what seems to be their right by holding a grudge or getting into unprofitable debates or arguments to prove they're right. They become weak so that the strength of God can work things out on their behalf. By doing so, they resist the devil with his temptations to argue, fuss, and hold a grudge. Because of this spirit of submission, the meek are free from these ill feelings. The meek gives the devil no soil in which to plant the seed of unforgiveness, so he must flee**.

> Submit yourselves, then, to God. Resist the devil, and he will flee from you.
> —James 4:7 (NIV)
>
> Guard the good deposit that was entrusted to you— guard it with the help of the Holy Spirit who lives in us.
> 2 Timothy 1:14 (NIV)
>
> Ye are of God, little children, and have overcome them: because greater is he that is in you, than he that is in the world.
> 1 John 4:4 (KJV)

Love the Lord with All Your Heart

> *Loving God with all our hearts means we love Him not solely in word but also most certainly in deed. Forgiving our offenders is one of those deeds.*

If we love God enough, we will come to love what He loves and hate what He hates. Therefore, what God loves will please us; thus, the thought, love God and do what pleases you. In doing what pleases us, we are doing what pleases God because we love Him; we love what He loves and hate what He hates.

Because of the love we have for God our Father, we cannot allow unforgiveness to linger in our spirit because that does not please Him. He hates that kind of conduct, so we should hate it as well. Remember, because we love Him, we come to love and hate what He loves and hates. We ought to hate unforgiveness because He hates unforgiveness.

We might be tempted to assert our rights and hold the offender responsible for what they have done to us until they apologize but our love for God should pull us back to a place of total surrender to the loving will of our Father.

Loving God with all our heart means we love Him not solely in word, but most certainly in deed. Forgiving our offenders is one of those deeds. To the naturally minded, this seems extremely difficulty, maybe even impossible. How could a person just forgive someone who has done them wrong? How could you just write off their offenses as if it never happened? Remember, the Holy Spirit is your Paraclete, your Helper, and Comforter. You can do it with His help.

Let us look at a few more Scriptures to get further understanding of the role of the Holy Spirit in helping us forgive our offender?

10. John 14:15-27— **The Holy Spirit will comfort us when we're hurting (John 14:18) and will bring us peace**.

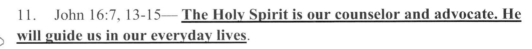

11. John 16:7, 13-15— **The Holy Spirit is our counselor and advocate. He will guide us in our everyday lives**.

12. Romans 8:1-17, 26— **The Holy Spirit will help us stop sinning and do the things that please God. Romans 8:26 tells us that the Holy Spirit helps us pray. The Holy Spirit intercedes for us. The Holy Spirit prays through us**.

13. Galatians 5:16-26— **"The fruit of the Spirit is love, joy, peace, patience, kindness, goodness, faithfulness, gentleness and self-control." The fruit of the Spirit should be evident in our lives. If we live by the Spirit, we should walk in the Spirit**.

You Can Do It

It is totally against our nature to forgive. When someone abuses us, emotionally, physically, or sexually; mars our reputation with rumors; or mistreats us in any way, it is not natural to forgive that person. Our natural inclination is to seek revenge, whether passive or active.

For us to forgive, we must put our will and our desires aside and listen to the counsel of the Holy Spirit. We know that although the Holy Spirit has come to comfort and guide us, that will not be the case if we do not give Him access. We must submit our will to God so we can forgive. You can do it!

End the session with prayer. Suggested prayer points:

1.   That God will reveal the areas of your life in which you still need to submit to Him.

2.   That God will give you a spirit of meekness.

3.   That God will increase your love for Him and that you will live out John 14:15 — *"If you love me, keep my commands."*

4.   For faith and confidence to believe that the Holy Spirit who lives in you is enough power for you to forgive.

Reflection and Personal Application

Read James 4:7— *"Submit yourselves, then, to God. Resist the devil, and he will flee from you"* — and think about it carefully. Meditate on it. Read it in several Bible versions. Read several commentaries to get a good understanding of what "submit to God" really means. The intent is for you to know what a life that is submitted to God looks like or how a person whose life is submitted to God would act toward their offender.

If you are in a situation where you need to forgive an offender, write down what you need to do to fully submit to God. Ask God for grace to submit these areas of your life to Him. This will empower you to forgive and reconcile with your offender.

> The power to foster inner healing is within you. You are not a helpless victim to the assaults of the enemy.

Session Goal

By the end of this session, participants will learn practical steps to emotional healing.

Prosper and Be in Health

Unforgiveness is the manifestation of emotional brokenness; therefore, the offended need healing. As believers, prayer is likely to be the first thing that comes to mind when we think of healing. There is no dispute there. Prayer is essential to our healing, but it does not stop there. After we have prayed — no matter how long or how intensely we've prayed — we must exit from our prayer closet and face life. After praying we must act in faith upon whatever we have asked of our heavenly Father. The actions we take in faith in our everyday lives are the real, practical steps to healing.

Seven practical steps to healing are as follows:

1. Face the truth.
2. Pray earnestly and in faith.
3. Depend on the Holy Spirit.
4. Obey the Word of God.
5. Stop defending yourself. Stop pointing fingers.
6. Receive the love of Christ.
7. Make the choice.

►Face the Truth

The unknown author of Crossing the River of Denial states, "Denial is the most cunning, baffling, and powerful part of my disease, the disease of alcoholism." While this is true of alcoholism, it is also true for any situation, including emotional ailments. If we are emotionally broken and we suppress the pain, telling ourselves nothing happened and that we are fine, we are in denial.

To start the healing process, we must face the fact that certain things challenge us. If we are in denial, we give God nothing to work with. Essentially, what we are saying is, nothing is wrong with us, we don't need healing.

When we face the facts, we become willing to talk about the issue. First, talk about it to yourself, and then talk about it to a trusted brother or sister. By talking about it with someone else, you break the silence and expose the enemy.

By breaking the silence, you break that death-sentence covenant you had with Satan. If you keep the secret between Satan and you, he has the power over you and can keep you captive. However, once you break the silence, you expose him, and his plan can no longer work as intended.

1. How does James 5:16 validate "Face the truth"? — **In order for healing to take place, we must break the death-sentence covenant between Satan and us. One depends on the other. We must tell someone.**

➢ *Discuss the word that in James 5:16.*

It cannot be easy to tell a sister in the Lord that you did not like her for years because you were jealous of her. Even so, I promise you, this bold step would not only benefit you, but it would bless the sister as well. It cannot be easy to confess to a brother or sister that you have spent years comparing yourself to him or her and always secretly tried to outdo him or her. It cannot be easy for a pastor to confess to a member of his ministerial staff that the member's spiritual gifts are threatening to him. It cannot be easy to confess to your pastor that you have undermined his plans and have blatantly disobeyed him because you have a controlling spirit; you feel like you're being told what to do, and you don't like it. None of these bold steps is easy, but scripture requires it. We are required to face the fact and confess our faults. That will position us for our healing.

A widely used strategy of the enemy is that he deceives us into believing there is no one in the Church or even in our

> Therefore confess your sins to each other and pray for each other so that you may be healed. The prayer of a righteous person is powerful and effective.
> —James 5:16 (NIV)

local assembly that we can trust. Therefore, many take the bait and believe that there is no one in the Church with whom they can share sensitive information. That is an absolute lie! If that were the case, God would not give us that command. I strongly urge you to face the fact, talk to yourself about your emotional issues, seek the Lord for guidance regrading who you can talk to, and He will take care of the rest.

▶ Pray Earnestly and in Faith

> *Prayer is one of the greatest privileges and absolutely the most powerful tool the body of Christ possesses, yet it is grossly underutilized.*

It is an awesome privilege to be able to approach our Father in prayer personally. We can go to Him anytime, anywhere, and with anything. He is always ready and willing to listen to us. We can pray all sorts of prayers — prayers of supplication, declaration, repentance, salvation, worship and praise, and warfare, and He hears them all. Prayer is one of the greatest privileges and absolutely the most powerful tool the body of Christ possesses, yet it is grossly underutilized.

Prayer is dialogue with our Father. It is a means of conversing with God, where both parties speak and both parties listen. Although we do not always hear from God while in prayer, we know He hears us and does answer in time. Prayer should be a natural part of our relationship with God. It should be something that occurs intuitively.

2. What do the following scriptures say about prayer?

    a. 1 Thessalonians 5:17— **Don't stop praying**.

    b. Jeremiah 33:3— **God will answer our prayers with things we know not of. He has the answers.**

c. Philippians 4:6-8— **Don't worry about anything. Pray about everything and God will give you peace that is beyond your understanding.**

d. Luke 18:1— **Don't grow weary in prayer. Pray always**.

e. 1 Peter 5:7— **If we give our cares to the Lord, he will take care of them. Our Father cares about us.**

f. We cannot lock ourselves in a prayer closet and stay on our knees in prayer, so how do we pray without ceasing? **The posture of our hearts and the state of our minds should always be in contact with our heavenly Father. We should not exclude Him from anything pertaining to us, even what seems to be the most minute thing. We should talk to Him about everything**.

> Pray without ceasing
> —1 Thessalonians 5:17 (KJV)
>
> Call unto me, and I will answer thee, and shew thee great and mighty things, which thou knowest not.
> —Jeremiah 33:3 (KJV)
>
> Then Jesus told his disciples a parable to show them that they should always pray and not give up.
> —Luke 18:1 (NIV)
>
> Casting all your care upon him; for he careth for you.
> —1 Peter 5:7 (KJV)

Our instinctive response to every situation should be consultation with our Father through prayer. Whenever we need help, our first recourse should be prayer. Therefore, you should talk to your Father about your emotional wounds. You may be the only one on earth who is knowledgeable of your emotional ailments, but your Father knows as well. He wants you to bring your cares to Him. He wants to heal you.

You can be brutally honest with Him. Nothing you say to Him will surprise Him. In fact, He wants you to be completely honest, totally open, bare, and naked before Him, so that He can clothe you with His joy, love, righteousness, and garment of gladness.

Pray sincerely until you get in His presence. Pray in faith, believing that He will answer your prayers. Do not doubt that He hears you. Do not doubt that He will respond with unconditional love, and you will enter His presence, where joy, healing, and restoration awaits you.

▶ Depend on the Holy Spirit

We can do absolutely nothing without the power of the Holy Spirit working in us. We must realize this and relinquish our will and strength to the Holy Spirit. The Holy Spirit came to lead us into all truth and to bring truth back to our memory (John 14:26).

The Holy Spirit is the agent that transforms our lives to become more like Christ. He is our teacher, guide, and empowering agent. The Holy Spirit can transform our lives beyond human comprehension or expectation.

The Holy Spirit operates well beyond human power. He operates in the supernatural to accomplish His will in our lives. Nothing and no one else can do this, so we must depend on the power of the Holy Spirit.

We get the power to resist sin and obey the Father solely from the Holy Spirit. Without Him, we will not have a genuinely fruitful and victorious Christian life. Similarly, we get the power we need to face our emotional wounds and deal with them in a healthy manner from the Holy Spirit. It is through the power of the Holy Spirit that we obtain our healing and deliverance. We must depend on the Holy Spirit and nothing else.

> Take heed to yourselves: If thy brother trespass against thee, rebuke him; and if he repent, forgive him. [4] And if he trespass against thee seven times in a day, and seven times in a day turn again to thee, saying, I repent; thou shalt forgive him. [5] And the apostles said unto the Lord, Increase our faith.
> —Luke 17:3-5 (KJV)
>
> He shall glorify me: for he shall receive of mine, and shall shew it unto you.
> —John 16:14 (KJV)
>
> For those who are led by the Spirit of God are the children of God.
> —Romans 8:14 (NIV)

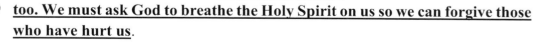

3. Discuss John 17:3-5. Why do you think the disciples asked Jesus to increase their faith right after he taught them about forgiveness? **They realized they need the help of the Holy Spirit to forgive, and we do too. We must ask God to breathe the Holy Spirit on us so we can forgive those who have hurt us**.

4. What else does depending on the Holy Spirit do for us?

    a.   John 16:14— **The Holy Spirit glorifies Christ through us**.

    b.   Romans 8:14— **He reveals the plan of God for us**.

    c.   Romans 8:15-16— **He assures us that we are children of God**.

God has so many wonderful plans for us. He told us in Jeremiah 29:11 that He has *"plans to prosper us and not to harm us, plans to give us hope and a future."* Then, in 3 John 2, we see that it is His desire that we enjoy good health and that all may go well with us, even as our soul prospers. Untended emotional hurt will rob us of the future of hope and the good holistic health that God has for us.

It is a blessed assurance to know that we are children of the only true God. There are members of the body of Christ who do not fully realize that they are children of God. They are not stepchildren or illegitimate children but children of His lineage, but they don't seem to know it. The devil uses the conditions of our lives, such as emotional brokenness, to disguise the truth and make us doubt our relationship to God. Nevertheless, the Holy Spirit came to lead us into truth such as this; we are children of God. We must fully depend on the Holy Spirit to obtain our healing and inherit the blessing that God has in store for us.

►Obey the Word of God

We will most definitely forfeit our healing if we walk in disobedience before God. To obtain emotional healing, we must obey God's Word.

5.   God has given us explicit instructions concerning the things we are to do to obtain emotional healing. For example:

    a.   James 5:16— **This Scripture tells us to *"confess our faults to one another, and pray for one another, that we may be healed."***

    b.   Matthew 5:44— **Specifically, God tells us to pray for our enemies and those who abuse and misuse us.**

    c.   Romans 12:14— **Bless and do not curse your enemies**.

    d.   Proverbs 17:9— **Seek love**.

> But I say unto you, Love your enemies, bless them that curse you, do good to them that hate you, and pray for them which despitefully use you, and persecute you;
> —Matthew 5:44 (KJV)
>
> Bless those who persecute you; bless and do not curse.
> —Romans 12:14 (NIV)
>
> Whoever would foster love covers over an offense, but whoever repeats the matter separates close friends.
> —Proverbs 17:9 (NIV)
>
> Turn from evil and do good; seek peace and pursue it.
> —Psalm 34:14 (NIV)
>
> If you love me, keep my commands.
> —John 14:15 (NIV)

e. Psalms 34:14— **Seek peace**.

f. Romans 12:18— **As much as we can do, live peacefully with everyone**.

6. What role does loving God play in our obedience to Him?

a. 1 John 5:3— **Love for God is to keep His commandments.**

b. John 14:15— **If we love God, we will keep His commandments**.

7. How does our love for God make us keep His commandment? **The secret to the strength and power we need to obey God is a sincere and untainted love for God. If we love God enough, we will obey Him, even when it hurts**.

▶ Stop Defending Yourself

The offended are always protecting themselves from further pain and hurt. When we are offended, we erroneously believe that we have a right to defend ourselves because no one should treat us in that manner. Nothing is wrong with caring for or securing the sanctity of our temples, but we often go wrong by defending ourselves. This objective is wrong because to defend ourselves, we must prove ourselves right and the other person(s) wrong. This is not always easy to do, which leaves the process at great risk of becoming distastefully ungodly.

> You were bought at a price. Therefore honor God with your bodies.
> —1 Corinthians 6:20 (NIV)
>
> You were bought at a price; do not become slaves of human beings.
> —1 Corinthians 7:23 (NIV)
>
> Do not take revenge, my dear friends, but leave room for God's wrath, for it is written: "It is mine to avenge; I will repay," says the Lord.
> —Romans 12:19 (NIV)
>
> I make known the end from the beginning, from ancient times, what is still to come. I say, 'My purpose will stand, and I will do all that I please.'
> —Isaiah 46:10 (NIV)

8. Why shouldn't we defend ourselves?

a. 1 Corinthians 6:20; 7:23— **We are not our own. God owns us**.

b. Romans 12:19— **God will take revenge for us. We don't have to do it**.

c. Isaiah 46:10— **Be still because God will do what He pleases. His purpose will stand**.

d. Exodus 14:14— **The Lord will fight for us; we just need to be still**.

e. Isaiah 54:17— **The plan of the enemy against you will not succeed, so no need to defend yourself**.

We belong to God the Father, and He is well able to take care of us. His thoughts toward us are good (Jeremiah 29:11). Therefore, as difficult as it may seem, we must operate as if we have no rights. We must be defenseless and allow God to fight our battles.

9. How did Jesus demonstrate this in the following scriptures?

a.   Isaiah 53:7— **When Jesus was oppressed, He didn't talk back**.

b.   Matthew 26:63— **Jesus remained silent when He stood before the high priest**.

c.   1 Peter 2:23— **When Jesus was reviled, He reviled not again.**

►Receive the Love of God

God has many names—peace, healer, provider, protector, and our righteousness, to name a few—but the one I believe describes Him to the fullest is *love*. Without love He would not heal, He would not provide, He would not protect, He would not give us peace, and He would not save us from our sins. God is love.

The price He paid for our sins, before we even knew we needed a Savior, speaks volumes about His love. His love is unconditional. We can do nothing to make Him love us any more or less than He already does. His love is complete. His love is comprehensive. It comes with all the added blessings that His Word describes.

Because of His love, God sent His Son *so that we might have life—and have it to the full*est (John 10:10 emphasis added). Contrary to what some may think, the abundant life that He came for us to have is to be experienced now. It is not just for when we reign with Him. We can enjoy this abundant life only if we walk in obedience to Him and if we live lives that entertain His presence.

Unaddressed or poorly addressed emotional wounds will forfeit our right to this abundant life.

When emotional wounds take residence in our spirits, we question our self-worth and could come to believe that God does not love us as He loves others.

God wants us to embrace His love. He wants us to know that He so loved the world—*He so loved everyone—that He gave His only Son to save us* (John 3:16 emphasis added), and that includes you.

> We love because he first loved us.
> —1 John 4:19 (NIV)
>
> The Spirit you received does not make you slaves, so that you live in fear again; rather, the Spirit you received brought about your adoption to sonship. And by him we cry, "Abba, Father."
> —Romans 8:15 (NIV)

10. What does the following passages of scripture say about receiving the love of God?

a.   1 John 4:19. **We love because He first loved us**.

b.   Romans 8:15. **When we receive the love of God, we know that we are His sons. Abba is our Father**.

c.   Revelation 3:20. **God loves us and wants to fellowship with us**.

►Make the Choice

Make the choice to declare the past is the past. Choose to take responsibility for your life today and for the rest of your days. Decide that you will no longer live in the past. You will no longer allow the past to influence your present. No longer will you leave your well-being and the quality of your life in the hands of anyone, let alone someone who has wronged you.

Make the choice to forgive. Forgiveness is a mandate from God, so your only choice is to forgive. However, you cannot forgive without the help of the Holy Spirit. Forgiving is an act of the will. If you do not allow the Holy Spirit to deal with you at the level of your will, you will be angry and sorry for yourself for the rest of your life.

You will never forgive if you wait until you feel like it. Submit yourself to God, and persistently resist the devil in his attempts to poison you with bitter thoughts. God your healer is ready to heal your wounded emotions once you take the first step towards forgiving your offender.

11. What will happen if you forgive others? (Matthew 6:12-14). **God will forgive you of your sins**.

> And forgive us our debts, as we forgive our debtors. [13] And lead us not into temptation, but deliver us from evil: For thine is the kingdom, and the power, and the glory, for ever. Amen. [14] For if ye forgive men their trespasses, your heavenly Father will also forgive you:
> —Matthew 6:12-14 (KJV)

This is a good enough reason to forgive *You can do it!*

End the session with prayer. Suggested prayer points:

1.   For strength to take the necessary steps to obtain emotional health.

2.   For a disciplined prayer life.

3.   For increased dependence on the Holy Spirit.

4.   For strength to obey the Word of God.

5.   For increased trust in the Lord and not in your own ways and understanding.

6.   That you will see yourself as God sees you and freely receive His unconditional love for you.

7.   For strength to make the right decisions — the decisions that line up with the Word of God — in all you do.

Reflection and Personal Application

Of the seven steps discussed in this chapter, write down the one that is most challenging for you. Try to think of the reason(s) why this is most challenging and write them down as well. Now find at least one Bible verse that speaks to each situation.

For example, if you find it difficult to stop defending yourself, you could read and meditate on Romans 12:19 or Exodus 14:14.

When you identify the verse for each challenge, read it in different Bible versions to get a good understanding of what the verse is saying. Pray the words in the verses in your prayers. By praying the Word of God, you cannot go wrong. It may be best to use an easily understood Bible version, such as the Amplified Version, the New International Version, the New English Translation, or the Living Bible.

Final Word

This brings us to the end of our discourse about forgiveness and the empowering grace of God to do so. These lessons contain a close look at what the Lord says about forgiveness, the blessings that are associated with forgiveness, and, inversely, the costs that are associated with unforgiveness. We also looked at the factors that are likely to increase the propensity for a person to be hurt and offended, why we handle hurt the way we do, and how we can obtain emotional healing. We ended with the reminder that with the help of the Holy Spirit that dwells in us, we can forgive.

Please know that you are now accountable for what you know, so by going through this study, you have canceled all your excuses for not forgiving those who have wronged you. Also know that although forgiving someone who offends you appears to be very difficult, maybe even impossible, our loving Father has not asked you to do anything He has not provided the grace for you to do. His grace is sufficient. That is the kind of God you serve. He is faithful. He does not set us up for failure. Do not forget that God has not asked you to do anything that He has not modeled for you either. He has empowered you to forgive. Your job is to activate the power that is within you.

Second Corinthians 12:9 says, "*My grace is sufficient for thee: for my strength is made perfect in weakness*" (KJV). This tells me that feeling like you cannot forgive your offender is not a bad place to be. In fact, you cannot forgive anyone. It is only through the Holy Spirit in you that you can forgive. When you feel like you cannot forgive your offender, you are, in fact, weak. In your weakness, you must relinquish all fleshy efforts and come under the power of God so that His strength can cover you. That is when He becomes strong—strong enough to empower you to do what you cannot do yourself.

I would like you to pause and think about the lessons you have gone through. I trust that what you have learned through these lessons has opened your spiritual eyes to discern the dynamics surrounding offense. Ask your heavenly Father to heighten your spiritual acuity and sharpen your recollection of what you have studied and the wisdom to practice it. The purpose of studying the lessons is to bring about change in your life. Do not miss that opportunity.

There is too much at stake not to forgive. You must forgive. It's a mandate from the God you love and serve. But the better news is that although it is difficult for you to do, with the help of the Holy Spirit, *you can*!

"The Lord bless you and keep you; [25] *the Lord make his face shine on you and be gracious to you;* [26] *the Lord turn his face toward you and give you peace."*
(Numbers 26:24-26, NIV)

Please consider leaving an honest and objective review of the book on Amazon.

Next book to be released: Church or God? Which One?

The question — Church or God? — is worth pondering and it deserves an honest answer that can only be found after prayerful introspection. To most Christians, church is a major part of our lives, and it should be. But how does church life — ministry, religious customs, relationships, events — rank with your relationship with God? To what degree have these and anything else related to church define the depth and vibrancy of your relationship with your God? Some Christians cannot imagine life without church. If that's you, this could be pointing to your answer to this very important question, but there is much more that must be taken into consideration before responding.

While fully acknowledging the God-ordained institution called church, Church Or God? Which One? will take you through an in-depth discourse of this question. This book details how we, God's beloved children, often unknowingly choose good things over our God, the absolute superior best. I will engage you in a thought-provoking discussion of why so many Christians seem to lose connection with God outside of the four walls of the church. The COVID-19 pandemic was a test of our allegiance to the God we serve. How does your relationship with God before and after the COVID-19 lockdown compare?

Endnotes

[1] Joyce Meyer, *Do Yourself A Favor... Forgive: Learn How to Take Control of Your Life through Forgiveness*. FaithWorks (2012).

[2] Jack W. Berry, Everett L. Worthington Jr., Les Parrott III, Lynn e. O'Connor, and Nathaniel G. Wade. "Dispositional Forgiveness: Development and Construct Validity of the Transgression Narrative Test of Forgiveness (TNTF)."

[3] Erick Messias, Anil Saini, Philip Sinato, and Stephen Welch, *Journal of Social Psychiatry and Psychiatric Epidemiology* (2010).

[4] Lynette Hoy, "Why Is It So Hard to Forgive?" Power to Change. http://powertochange.com/discover/life/forgivehard/

[5] Everett L. Worthington, "The New Science of Forgiveness," (September 2004). https://greatergood.berkeley.edu/article/item/the_new_science_of_forgiveness#gsc.tab=0

[6] Charlotte vanOyen Witvliet, Thomas E. Ludwig, and Kelly L. Vander Laan, "Granting forgiveness or harboring grudges: Implications for emotion, physiology, and health," *Psychological Science* 12, no. 2 (2001).

[7] Loren L. Toussaint, Davis R. Williams, Marc A. Musick, and Susan A. Everson-Rose, "Why forgiveness may protect against depression: Hopelessness as an explanatory mechanism," *Personality and Mental Health* 12, no. 2 (2008): 89–103.

[8] Everett L. Worthington Jr. and Michael Scherer. "Forgiveness is an emotion-focused coping strategy that can reduce health risks and promote health resilience: theory, review, and hypotheses." *Psychology and Health* 19, no. 3 (2007): 385–405.

Made in the USA
Middletown, DE
07 March 2023

26372446R00091